A COP'S

By Dominic
and John V. Piatersen, Jr.

What Rats Will Do
Cronyism at its Worst

Corruption and Dysfunctional Incompetence
The Erie County, Pennsylvania Judicial System

The Front Cover:

The drawing of the Lady Liberty was made in May 1993 by Patrick J. DiPaolo. Son of Dom and Janet, days after Judge DiPaolo won his first election. Pat was an Art Teacher at this time in the Erie School District, assigned to Roosevelt Junior High.

The framed drawing hung in Judge DiPaolo's Courtroom for 24 years.

Published by: BADGE 88 PRODUCTIONS, LLC.

Erie, Pennsylvania

Copyright © 2020 Dominick D. DiPaolo

ISBN: 978-1-63877-913-1

Library of Congress Control Number: 2014936914

Printed in the United States of America.

DEDICATION

To my family:

Again, this work could not have existed without the continued support. Patience and love of my wife Janet, and our children Patrick J. DiPaolo and Dawn DiPaolo-Romeo who were all effected by my position in Law Enforcement and my Judicial Career for fifty years in Erie County Pennsylvania.

They have been there for me through all of life's joys and tribulations, and will forever be my source of great pride, strength and love.

God Bless You.
Love Always,

Dominick

Dedicated in Loving Memory of Our Beloved Son

Patrick John DiPaolo

1969-2013
"Our Hero"
Thank you for being our son.

WIEITOT

SOURCING, METHODOLOGY & OPINION VS. FACT

Factual information contained herein was culled from police records, court documents and transcripts, statements of victims, witnesses and defendants, notes, newspaper clippings and other sources of public and private information. At times material was obtained from Dominick D. DiPaolo's memory.

Opinion and private thoughts have been clearly identified as those of the author, or are obvious to the reader. On rare occasions where no written or oral record, or gaps in the storyline exit, dramatic license is taken and reasonable supposition employed.

As always, every person charged with or suspected of a crime is considered not guilty until proven otherwise through court conviction or guilty plea.

Author's note: In writing this book, my intent was to no way attack or malign all members of the Judicial System – District Attorneys, PA Office of Attorney General, United States Attorneys, F.B.I. Agents, Judges, their staffs or Police Officers. The overwhelming majority of these public officials are neither corrupt nor incompetent. Yet I believe the references to those mentioned here – part of the federal, state and Erie County Judicial System – to be true, correct or the result of my honest and considered personal and profession opinion, based on usually reliable information encountered during my decades of public service.

WHO'S WHO

The list of names contained of every person identified within the following pages according to the positions they held or were known by during the time frame referenced. Many of them on this list clearly have been involved in the criminal and civil justice system, others are respected in the criminal and civil justice systems, or mentioned in passing with various connections to the central theme, some important, some innocuous as the story unfolds through the many twists and turns of these investigations and incidents that occurred in Erie, Pennsylvania in the Court System. Readers should not infer wrongdoings merely because an individual is listed in this book. The author intentions is to provide readers with positive resources, helpful in identifying the individuals who are in this book.

A

Aaron, Tom - Erie County Court Administrator
Abate, Frank - Erie County District Judge
Abeb-Ali, Ammed - Arrested for dealing drugs
Acri, Mike - Boxing Promoter
Adams, A.J. - Erie Attorney, Former Assistant Public Defender
Agresti, Chuck - Erie Attorney, Solicitor F.O.P.
Agresti, Richard "Dick" - Erie Attorney, Founder of Boys Baseball in Erie
Aldrete, Hank - Erie Detective
Alonge, Gerald - Erie County District Judge
Altadonna, Denise - Sister of Shelly and Frank Altadonna
Altadonna, Frank V. - DiPaolo's former PA State Constable
Altadonna-Banta, Shelly - DiPaolo's former secretary
Amicangelo, Andrea - Northwest Legal Services
Andrezeski, Anthony "Buzz" - PA State Senator

B

Badams, Dr. Jay - Erie School District Superintendent
Bagnoni, David M. - DiPaolo's Detective partner, Airport Police Chief
Bagnoni, Mario S. - Erie Deputy Chief of Police, Erie City Councilman
Barker, Dr. James - Erie School District Superintendent
Barnes, Kenneth - Convicted murder
Baxter, Lou - News Director at WJET Erie, PA
Berardi, Art - Erie Police Commissioner
Biden, Joseph R. - U.S. President

Bizzarro Family - Boxing Promoters
Blackburn Detective Agency (Nationwide)
Borzillieri, Trey - Director TMZ
Bowers, Jr., Charles - Erie Policeman
Bowers, Sr., Charles - Chief of Police, Erie Police Department
Bozza, John - Erie County Judge
Brooks, Scott - F.B.I. Agent
Brzezinski, Ed - Erie School District Director
Buchanan, Mary Beth - US Attorney , Pittsburgh, PA
Bush, George W. - United States President

C

Cannavino, Arthur "Skip" - Erie City Treasurer
Cannavino, Michael - Erie City Councilman, Mayor elect
Cappabianca, Italo - PA State Representative
Cappabianca, Linda - Italo's wife
Carlson, John - Erie Attorney
Carney, Tom - Erie County District Judge
Casey Jr., Bob - US Senator
Casey Sr., Bob - PA Governor
Catagirone, Thomas - PA State Rep, Chairman of Judiciary Committee
Cessar, Robert - Interim US Attorney, Pittsburgh, PA
Chase, Emory - PA Bondsman
Chase, Robert - Erie County District Attorney
Chimenti, Armand - Chief of Police, Erie Police Department
Cimino, David J. - PA State Constable
Clark, Danielle - Jerry Clark's wife
Clark, Jerry - F.B.I. Agent
Clark, Ramsey - U.S. Attorney General
Clinton, Bill - U.S. President
Colosimo, Kevin - Pittsburgh PA Attorney
Connelly, Shad - Erie County Judge
Coraban, Paul - Newspaper reporter
Corbett, Tom - PA Attorney General, PA Governor
Cousins, John "Jack" - Deputy Chief of Detective, Erie, PA
Covatto, Al - CEO Telatron, DiPaolo's cousin
Covatto, Michael - CEO Unicredit of America, Al's son
Cunningham, William "Rusty" - Erie County District Attorney, Erie
    County Judge
Curtis, Scott - I.R.S. Agent

D

E

F

G

H

Hagmann, Doug - Private Investigator
Hahn, Tim - News Reporter
Hammer, Scott - Erie County District Judge
Harkins, Pat - PA State Representative
Hawk, Michelle - Erie Attorney
Heibel, Grace - Brad Foulk's grandmother
Heibel-Foulk, Jean - Brad Foulk's mother
Hickton, David - US Attorney, Pittsburgh
Hill, Elaine - Judge Fabrizi's sister and secretary
Hoffa Sr., Jimmy - Vanished Union Leader
Holder, Eric - U.S. Attorney General
Hoover, J. Edgar - Director of F.B.I.
Howard, Pat - Newspaper Reporter

J

Jones, Alex - Radio host
Joyce, Michael - Erie County Judge, convicted of insurance fraud,
    Federal prison
Juliante Sr., Jess - Erie County Judge

K

Kallenbach, Kevin - Erie Attorney, Assistant Public Defender
Kennedy, John F. - U.S. President
Kennedy, R. Gordon - Erie County District Attorney
Killen, Jeffery - Chief Counsel for F.B.I.
Kimerer, Hannibal - U.S. Senator Specter's Chief of Staff
King, Don - TVKO Boxing Promoter
Kirk, Jeannie - murder victim
Kruszewski, Michael - Erie Attorney
Kuhn, Bob - Erie Policeman
Kuhn, Maggie - Erie Policewoman
Kuhn, Norm - Erie Police Detective
Kurzwicz, Matt- Pittsburgh Attorney
Kurzwicz, Pete - Pittsburgh Attorney
Kwitowski, Frank - Captain of Detectives, Erie Police

L

Lashinger, Christine - Sued for bad debt

N

Nash, Gary - Erie Attorney
Nygard, Richard - Erie County Judge, U.S. Federal Judge

O

Oaks Vendetti, Laurie - John Vendetti's wife
Obama, Barack - U.S. President
Oblerman, Keith - National News Reporter
Orlando, Greg - Erie Stockbroker
Orlando, Nancy - Greg Orlando's wife

P

Palattella, Ed - Erie Times News Reporter sued by DiPaolo
Paolello, Anthony - Convicted of murder and rape
Pasquale, Luigi - Operations Manager of Erie County
Pasquale, Tony - News Reporter
Pella, Carol - Investigative news reporter
Petrunger Jr., Frank - Erie School Director
Pfadt, William - Erie County Judge
Piccinni, Marshall - Assistant U.S. Attorney
Pinski, Jeff - Editor Erie Morning News
Pitonyak, Jim - Erie Attorney
Placidi, Gene "Jeep" - Bagnoni Campaign Chairman
Polito, Brian - Superintendent Erie Public Schools

R

Reed Ward, Paula - News Reporter Pittsburgh
Rendell, Ed - PA Governor
Reymore, Daria - Erie Business Owner
Reymore, Larry - Erie Business Owner
Richmond, Hyle - News TV Reporter
Ridge, Tom - U.S. Congressman, PA Governor, Secretary Homeland Security
Rivera, Geraldo - FOX National News
Robinson, Eugene - National News Reporter
Romeo, Gianna - DiPaolo's granddaughter
Romeo, Gino - DiPaolo's grandson
Romeo, Michael - DiPaolo's son-in-law
Rotunda, Frank - Erie Policeman, convicted felon
Rudge, Bob - Agent In Charge F.B.I. (Erie)

S

T

U

V

Valentta, Marlene - Victim of rape and beating
Vendetti, Angeline - Mother of John Vendetti
Vendetti, John - Erie County District Judge
Veschecco, Michael - Erie County District Attorney
Vogel, Jim - Assistant District Attorney, Stanley Murder Prosecutor
Vogt, Helen - Murder victim
Vogt, Herbert "Hubby" - Helen's Husband - Golf Pro
Vorscheck Sr., Bill - DiPaolo's boss at GE

W

Wagner, Paul - Erie TV News Reporter
Walnuts, Paulie - Soparano Gang
Walczak, Joe - Erie City Councilman
Washburn, Jim - Erie Detective, DiPaolo's partner
Watts, Mark - Erie County Detective
Wecht, Dr. Cyril - Allegheny County Coroner
Weichler, Bill - Erie Attorney
Weindorf, Joe - Erie Police Detective, Erie County District Judge
Wells, Brian - Murder victim, Pizza Bomber
Williamson, Charles - City of Erie Mayor
Wilson, Andrew - F.B.I. Agent
Wolf, Tom - PA Governor
Wright, Don - Erie Attorney
Wright, Gail - PA State Representative

TABLE OF CONTENTS

CHAPTER 1

IN THE BEGINNING: ERIE'S LITTLE ITALY DiPAOLO FAMIGLIA

Appropriately arriving under the Sagittarius symbol of the archer and the element of fire, Dominick D. DiPaolo was born in Erie, Pennsylvania, December 18, 1946, to Pasquale "Pat" and Vincenza Mary "Babe" Pallotto DiPaolo. One of the first of the Baby Boom generation, Dominick had an older sister, Patty, who was just six at the time.

Erie was then Pennsylvania's third largest city, with a population approaching 150,000, and situated on Lake Erie, halfway between Cleveland, Ohio, and Buffalo, New York, 100 miles from each, and roughly 130 miles north of the nation's steel capital, Pittsburgh, Pa.

A city of immigrants from the previous century and early in the 20th century, Erie now boasted the successful second and third generation families of those immigrants.

The DiPaolo family, for example, had settled in Erie's "Little Italy," a self-contained city within a city inhabited mostly by this first- and second-generation Italian Americans, and by Italian immigrants who arrived in the United States earlier, passing through Ellis Island, awestruck by their ship's closeness to the Statue of Liberty, on their way west to Northwestern Pennsylvania. Dominick's parents' families were from Southern Italy, his dad's family from Rocca Pia, a province of L'Aquila in Abruzzi; his mom's Pallotto family from Montenero Val Cocchiara, a province of Isernia in Molise.

"Little Italy" was unique in Erie. Although pockets of ethnic immigrants were scattered throughout the city, most notably the Poles on the lower eastside and Russians along the Bayfront, where strong young men worked the docks and Eastern Orthodox onion-domed churches appeared, "Little Italy" was a much more well-defined geographical region.

It had its own mostly Roman Catholic churches, both parochial and public schools, stores, intoxicating aroma-producing bakeries, bars, clubs, movie houses, factories and even funeral parlors. English, broken English and Italian were spoken, often in the same sentence.

Many of the residents of "Little Italy" did not own cars. There was no need to. The men of that era and area walked to work at Marx Toys, commonly called "The Monkey Works," Continental Rubber, Erie Forge, Griswold Manufacturing, and other "shops" not far from their small, well-kept homes, flats or apartments. For jobs out of "Little Italy," the Erie Coach Company buses provided dependable transportation to any location in town. Women generally were stay-at-home moms, often attending morning mass and making sure their family's spiritual needs were met.

Life was often hard, but most did not seem to mind their lack of materialistic lifestyles. They were free, productive and had become well-assimilated in their new land of opportunity. Families were the glue that held "Little Italy" together as a strong, cohesive community. Already, in just a few short decades, Erie's Italian Americans were already making great inroads into the professions, becoming doctors, lawyers, educators, many answering the calling of religious community to become priest and nuns. (Today, not much remains to justify the name in that geographical community. It is still called "Little Italy," but the reasons for that designation disappeared long ago as attrition and upper-mobility to other areas claimed most of the Italian residents.)

But into the post-WWII era and that now-departed way of life came the DiPaolos. The family occupied a second-floor flat at 926 W. 18th Street, owned by Joe and Philomenia DiFucci, who lived downstairs with their four children, Ralph, Marie, Esther and Pasquale, nick-named "Sonny."

First generation Americans Pat DiPaolo and Joe DiFucci were living what they called "The American Dream." They had family-sustaining jobs in local factories, and were doing better than they had it in their upbringing by immigrant parents struggling during the Great Depression.

Pat worked at the sprawling General Electric plant, building locomotives. He lied about his age to get the job at age 15 to help out at home, then worked for GE for the next 45 years. The job provided an opportunity for him to also become active in union politics, as well as Erie's hotbed of Democratic Party politics. Joe worked at National Forge, not far away.

Mary, meanwhile, was a stay-at-home wife and mom, raising her children in the same way as most Italian women of that era: The papa worked; the mama had domain over the home and kids. That's simply the way it was, and although it is a generalization, many, if not most, seemed happy and content with the generations-long arrangement.

Erie in the post-war 1940s and 1950s, also was as political as any much larger city of the day, often divided by its main street – State Street – as eastside/westside, Polish/Italian. As a result, it did not take long for Pat to become fascinated by and absorbed into the bustling local political scene.

While Pat never actually stood for any elected political office, he was known throughout the area for his keen organizational skills, especially when he applied that savvy to political campaigns in the Democratic Party. The first campaign Pat managed in 1950 resulted in the election of his good friend, Mike Cannavino, to the office of Erie City Assessor. Cannavino would evolve into one of the most successful and powerful politicians in Erie history, and also one of the most colorful, serving as a City Councilman and ultimately becoming the Democratic nominee for mayor in 1965.

Cannavino was considered a shoo-in to win the general election against one-term incumbent Republican Charles Williamson, and likely would have easily won against Williamson and his unpopular administration. But the like able Cannavino suffered a fatal heart attack only slightly more than a week prior to Election Day.

Just the day before Mike was found dead in the downtown Lawrence Hotel room where he lived, he had spent the evening with Pat DiPaolo at the Knights of St. John's, a popular westside Erie club, during a political meeting.

As the Democratic Party's Third Ward chairman in Erie's "Little Italy" for 25 years, Pat DiPaolo was considered by many to be the westside's "King Maker," with the ability to help not only budding and established politicians, but also the average folks in obtaining work and starting political careers. Prior to the 1970s, government jobs were not governed by labor unions, but by political patronage. Politicians controlled who got hired to what job. Locally, ward chairs were powerful political positions and had the absolute power to approve or deny government job applications. Unionization of government workers in Pennsylvania took hold, however, under Governor Milton Shapp, the first Jewish governor of the Commonwealth and also the first governor to hold two terms under the recently revised state constitution. Pat also got involved in many civic organizations, including "The Marconi Club," made up of Italian men who worked together with Erie city police officers to form the Police Athletic League, or simply the PAL, as it was known. The group was known for getting involved in the lives of kids living in poverty, and those perhaps headed in the wrong direction, and then becoming a positive influence in the youngsters' lives before it was too late for them.

As young Dominick DiPaolo grew older, he took advantage of some of the athletic avenues made available to him, such as organized baseball. Youth baseball in Erie had been founded by Attorney Richard Agresti, and the movement worked hand-in-hand with the PAL organization, each helping to get and keep kids off Erie's mean streets, no matter which side of town they resided.

Decades earlier, a short physical distance, but far removed in reality from that idyllic southwest Erie neighborhood where he would one-day make his family home, young Dominick DiPaolo knew he wanted to be a cop. It's rare that our childhood dreams and wishes one day become reality. But not in this case. In fact, as far back as he could remember, DiPaolo wanted to be a police officer. A good cop.

In those seemingly innocent days of the 1950s, days before the Camelot-associated Kennedy Administration, there was no visceral loathing of the U.S. Federal Bureau of Investigation, or the U.S. Attorney's Office. A kid growing up during that decade would have little or no understanding, other than what he saw in the movies or TV shows, of what either agency was responsible for accomplishing.

Yet, events that transpired over the coming years and decades had a way of altering perceptions, those which are imagined, and those which are mostly true.

To understand why and what altered those perceptions, one merely must allow historical facts and records speak clearly for themselves. To even better understand the present, it is often imperative to travel back to another era – to the immediate post-World War II era – to a time when perceptions prevailed; perceptions mattered.

Here's the what; and better, yet, the why...

CHAPTER 2

THE 1950S: COPS, POLITICS IMPRESSIONS

There is little doubt Dominick DiPaolo's early years were greatly influenced by police and politics, an influence that would later motivate him to become not only one of Erie's finest, but also to get involved in local politics, especially in Erie's vast Sixth Ward. Politics or not, he wanted to help others, just as those in the Police Athletic League did.

DiPaolo's life as the son of a Democratic Party ward chairman provided an education most others his age could not even begin to imagine. After Dominick graduated from Technical Memorial High School, he worked at the General Electric Company's Erie plant – Building No. 10, where locomotive assembly took place – alongside his dad. He also became successfully involved with U.E. Local 506 as a union steward. But the younger DiPaolo held onto his dream of one day becoming a cop, and eventually he was afforded the opportunity to take the official Civil Service test, a requirement for all those desiring "To Protect and Serve." He did well.

He had worked in the east Erie GE "shop" for four years, was now married to Janet Colao and they were expecting their first child, Patrick, in 1969, when the incredible news arrived: He had been appointed an Erie Police officer. He was on jury duty, picked for a murder trial, and phoned Janet to request clothes as the jury would be sequestered. She quickly told him of the registered letter that arrived from the City of Erie Bureau of Police.

After telling her to open the letter and learning of the appointment, he informed the tip staff and was taken before the judge to explain what had transpired. Both the District Attorney and defense attorney excused him from jury duty.

But Pasquale DiPaolo did not want his son to be a cop. He was worried, perhaps for good reason, about the younger DiPaolo's safety. In a last ditch political effort to thwart the move, Pasquale used his connections to arrange for an inner-plant transfer and promotion of sorts for his son.

Bill Vorsheck Sr., Dominick DiPaolo's foreman, called the young man into his office. He told DiPaolo he knew of the pending arrival of the young couple's first child and offered to transfer DiPaolo to Building 90, the Personnel Department, where he would have a white collar position at an annual salary of $6,300 – far more than he was making on the assembly line.

At once, DiPaolo understood what was happening: Vorsheck and Pat DiPaolo were best pals. This had to be Pat's move to prevent Dominick from becoming a cop. DiPaolo recalls the great job Bill did trying to discourage him from leaving General Electric, but the young man with the growing family was now more determined than ever. A short time later, he left GE and was sworn in as a City of Erie policeman at an annual salary of $4,900.

DiPaolo's earlier brushes with politics, as well as Pasquale's keen political influence in his son's life, would serve DiPaolo well throughout his law enforcement career. He would put his political acumen to good use over the coming years to help many others. But never himself.

And he would make Pasquale and Mary proud.

CHAPTER 3

THE EARLY YEARS ON THE ERIE POLICE DEPARTMENT

Dom DiPaolo started his career at the Erie Police Department as a Patrolman like every other Rookie. The amount of money Policemen made having them take as many off duty jobs as possible, called "Moonlighting".

DiPaolo quickly took as many jobs as he could to support his young family. And he had a home for he and his wife Janet that they had built with the help of his father. Janet, prior to son Patrick's birth, worked full time as a beautician, but then stayed home raising Patrick, and then their daughter Dawn.

One of the jobs DiPaolo had was the Boston Store Cafeteria. In the early 70s, that was the hangout for high school and college kids after school. Hundreds of young people gathered there five days-a-week, and he kept the peace in uniform.

Every Monday the Policeman got paid and you had to go to the accounting department on the sixth floor to get your check.

One day the checks weren't ready so DiPaolo, who was off that day in street clothes, went down to the Boston Store cafeteria to wait.

While he was there having a pop, he was approached by a young man who sat down with him and started up a conversation. The guy was going to Gannon and was from the Pittsburgh, and he offered DiPaolo a nickel bag of smoke. ($5.00 bag of marijuana). Naturally in the early 70's, marijuana was just coming in all over and there were many people dealing.

DiPaolo told the guy, I don't have any money on me, but I can get some and made arrangements to meet back in an hour.

DiPaolo went to the Police Department across the street and told the man in charge what happened. He called Sergeant's Chuck Erickson and Pat Shanahan who were in charge of the Narcotics and Intelligence Unit. They asked DiPaolo, who was then 22-year-old, if he would make a Controlled Buy from this guy.

DiPaolo said he would. So they gave him a marked five dollar bill and he met the guy and made the buy. Erickson and Shanahan grabbed him as the guy left the Boston Store, and arrested him.

DiPaolo had been on the Police Force for eleven months and was called into the Chiefs office the next day when he reported for duty. Chief Armand Chimenti, and Sergeant's Erickson and Shanahan who were also there, asked DiPaolo if he would work with the Drug Unit and go undercover. DiPaolo didn't hesitate. He learned the kid from Pittsburgh was the son of a Judge and was a major dealer at Gannon.

That was the break DiPaolo caught in his young career. For the next few year, he made many buys in the Erie Community from drug dealers of all ages.

When he got burned out (people putting out the word who he was), he was part of the Drug Enforcement Unit as a detective. Then he was transferred to the Detective Division investigating all types of cases.

He investigated his first murder at age 23 and stayed in the Detective Division his entire career. He was the youngest policeman to become a Detective.

Chief Chimenti retired later and Charles Bowers, Sr. became the Chief. Now assigned to the Detective Division, DiPaolo was called into Bowers office.

Bowers advised DiPaolo that he talked with Lt. Phil Lupo of the Criminal Investigation Division and requested a Detective for a special assignment, and Lupo recommended DiPaolo. It was then on the daily detail DiPaolo was assigned special duty to the Chiefs office, with no further information.

Bowers explained: A neighbor of his who worked as a Security Guard at a hospital told Bowers a City Cop working third shift would come to the hospital and meet with a Resident Physician and they both would visit women who just gave birth and perform intimate examination in their rooms all hours of the night. He further advised the Cop donned scrubs to impersonate a doctor.

Bowers told DiPaolo "Take these two "Mother Fucken Perverts" down as fast as you can.

DiPaolo not knowing who the cop was checked the third shift detail and observed who the beatman was and who was in the district car covering the hospital. He set up a surveillance and knew the emergency room doors were the only ones open after 9 P.M. So he set up there. He sat two nights with no Cops going in. The third night he observed the Beat Cop go into the hospital at 12:30 A.M. and walked back out at 3:00 A.M.

DiPaolo the next day called the Cop in and advised him he was aware of his deception and illegal activities with the examination of the women at the hospital. The Cop caved in and started crying and gave a statement.

DiPaolo had already prepared two documents. The first an arrest warrant and the second a letter of resignation.

"Take your pick," he told the cop. The Cop wanted to discuss his options with his uncle, a member of the department's brass, but DiPaolo refused to allow it, thus forcing the resignation. Bowers, meanwhile, knowing the relationship between the dirty Cop and ranking Office, immediately took the resignation letter to the personnel office for processing.

"Bowers didn't want some shit to change it," DiPaolo recalled. "But the shit did hit the fan when Mayor Lou Tullio found out. Not only was the dirty Cop's uncle brass, but another uncle was a City Councilman."

Yet the resignation went through and the Cop was finished on the force. The Mayor was livid with both Bowers and DiPaolo.

DiPaolo then went to the hospital and the Resident Doctor at once lawyered up. In fact, DiPaolo learned that prior to him trying to talk to the Doctor, his Lawyer Attorney Jess Juliante already called the Mayor and advised he was going to be sent out of town "for counseling". The D.A. suggested blowing him into the PA Medical Board which DiPaolo gladly did.

About six months later, the ex-cop was working in the Erie Streets Department, thanks to his political pull. Big Lou was pissed as he wasn't able to control the situation.

A few years later, the Doctor came back to Erie and over the years, DiPaolo heard stories about him being involved with illegal drugs. But it could not have been just rumors? Yeah Right! DiPaolo believes the Doctor is now retired or moved out of Erie.

DiPaolo who also had a "moonlighting" job on the door at the Calabrese Club which was the go to place on the weekends until 3:00 A.M. He was working when the ex-cop came in all drunked up. DiPaolo said to him... I think you better come back another night and you don't need anymore drinks tonight.

The ex-cop stated you fucked me out of my job and now you're going to break my ball in front of my girlfriend? DiPaolo told him first off, you fucked yourself over your job and you've had enough to drink already.

The guy started to yell and swear and DiPaolo said you are embarrassing yourself and if you keep it up, you're going to get locked up. The girl he was with pleaded with him to leave and he did.

Over the years, they would see each other at the City Garage (Streets Department) as this is where all the Police cars got their gas. But nothing was ever said. The ex-cop never returned to the Cally Club when DiPaolo was on the door.

CHAPTER 4

NO JUSTICE FOR HELEN VOGT

In 1988, there was a murder investigation of Helen Vogt, a 77-year-old brutally beaten and stabbed many times about her head and face. Her husband, Herbert "Hubby" Vogt, was a golf pro who ran the Erie Golf Course for years, had died just prior to this attack. DiPaolo, and his partner, Jim Washburn, quickly developed a prime suspect and traveled to Texas in an attempt to interview him.

When the Erie cops, along with Texas law enforcement officers, arrived unannounced at the suspect's home, they were greeted by the man's mother, who said her son was not at home. While the officers and the mom chatted at the front door, the door to the attached garage opened and the suspect sped out and away on a motorcycle.

Yet, within a short time, DiPaolo and Washburn, along with the Texas officers, arranged for the parents to bring their murder suspect son to the local police department to meet with the Erie contingent.

To the police officers' surprise, the suspect showed up with an attorney; so did his parents. The detectives knew they had their man; why else would the parents lawyer up?

As expected, the suspect's attorney advised his client not to answer questions. Yet, with the information the Erie detectives developed, there was enough probable cause to secure a search warrant to obtain the suspect's fingerprints. Texas law enforcement officers served the warrant, based on information received from DiPaolo and Washburn. As a result, a major set of prints (full hands and palms) were taken from the suspect as his lawyer stood by.

Meanwhile, the Erie cops were attempting to speak with the suspect's parents, but their attorneys would not permit it, either. All this indicated to DiPaolo that he and Washburn had hit the jackpot. But – while being printed, the suspect suddenly asked Washburn, "Does Pennsylvania have a death penalty?"

"Shut your mouth!" his lawyer interjected.

But Washburn replied, "We sure do!"

With the prints in hand, the Erie detectives headed home. DiPaolo immediately phoned the DA's office and attempted to reach John Bozza, the assistant District Attorney assigned to the case. But, since Bozza was in court, DiPaolo asked to speak directly to District Attorney Cunningham.

Once he got the DA on the phone, he quickly brought Cunningham up to speed on the case: the trip to Texas, the suspect and parents "lawyering" up, the death penalty comment. It was DiPaolo's idea to bring the parents to Erie to testify before the grand jury. Since the target of the probe could not be taken to the grand jury, DiPaolo still reasoned that the parents might fold and make his case. He knew he had hit a nerve with both the suspect and his parents, and with the grand jury seated in Erie County, and being run by Assistant District Attorney Brad Foulk, appeared the best way forward.

Cunningham told DiPaolo his plan could be discussed when he got back to Erie.

Later, after days of discussions, Cunningham and Foulk told DiPaolo and Washburn they had talked with the parents' Texas attorneys. If subpoenaed, the Texas lawyers said, the parents would show up, but plead "The Fifth" – their Constitutional right against self-incrimination.

"Great!" DiPaolo said. "Bring them to the grand jury, let them take the Fifth, and then grant them immunity from prosecution. You know they are aware of what the son did." Then if they don't testify, they go to jail.

DiPaolo further told the local D.A.s: "We all know that the parents were in Texas when the son committed this murder and that he had to tell them – that's why they all won't talk. We got him!"

But Cunningham and Foulk pointed to the cost of bringing the parents from Texas to Erie. The transportation, food and lodging costs. And what if the parents don't know anything? the D.A.s asked.

When DiPaolo protested, pointing out the parents would not have lawyered-up if they did not have valuable information about the case, the two lawyers, Cunningham and Foulk, said bringing the parents to Erie County was simply too risky.

"Bullshit!" DiPaolo said replied.

DiPaolo and Washburn were livid. Both knew from the reactions of the parents and the suspect that the cops had Helen Vogt's killer. But there was nothing they could do about it.

There is other information on this case which DiPaolo will not give up, as this is still an active case. But he and Washburn know the suspect did not come to Erie alone and are convinced the parents knew who the other guy was.

Still, for months DiPaolo complained bitterly to ADA Bozza. But Bozza said Cunningham and Foulk were not convinced the detectives had the right guy. For one, they could not match the suspect's prints to any at the crime scene, which had been wiped down. Mrs. Vogt's car, taken after the murder and abandoned at a Greyhound Bus Station's parking lot in Dayton, Ohio, also had been wiped clean.

"So what!" DiPaolo countered. "All investigations would be easy if you had prints at every crime scene!" He believed that the grand jury was the most valuable tool in solving crimes by using the immunity, or the threat of perjury charges, to elicit testimony. He knew what happened in Chicago and New York when mobsters were given immunity. They quickly caved on their pals and bosses even family members. Law enforcement in those locales did not see grand juries as being "too risky." In fact, DiPaolo had first-hand experience on the value of grand juries with the "Ash Wednesday" hired hit involving Caesar Montevecchio and his boys.

"Thanks to Cunningham and Foulk," DiPaolo would later say, "this killer walked."

DiPaolo recalled that Cunningham had gone to Erie County Executive Judy Lynch seeking $30,000 to seat a countywide grand jury. "He made her believe a number of unsolved murders would go before the panel, including Helen Vogt's," DiPaolo said.

According to DiPaolo, Cunningham explained to Lynch that grand juries can be useful tools in stalled investigations because the panels can compel witnesses to testify under threat of legal penalties. It was exactly what DiPaolo had wanted to do.

"This is the same theory I told him about our suspect in Texas, especially concerning the suspect's parents. But it fell upon deaf ears for whatever reason and he and Foulk balked," DiPaolo said.

But DiPaolo, like many dedicated cops, refused to let the matter simply drop. In fact, from 1988 until 2019, for more than 30 years, DiPaolo kept tabs on the suspect. He found the suspect served much time in jail, the last arrest being for bank robberies in the South. He is still serving time.

"You would think," DiPaolo would later say, "that as a cold case that our police would want to solve and bring justice to the Vogt family, the Erie Police Department would open the cold case, learn what jails this guy occupied, who his cellmates or co-defendants were, and if he ever spoke about a murder he committed 30 years ago in Erie, Pennsylvania. It's called good police work. But in the meantime, there's been no justice for Helen Vogt."

During his 25-year police career, DiPaolo arrested 2,006 people. Hundreds of them went to prison. Some plead guilty. Others were found guilty by a jury. But hundreds of these criminals did not leave their fingerprints at the scenes of crimes. DiPaolo could still not believe that two D.A.s would allow a suspect to walk because his prints were not found at the murder scene.

CHAPTER 5

ATTORNEY GUS McGEORGE SHOT AND CHARGED

In February 1988, Erie lawyer Gus McGeorge was shot in the chest in his office by Henry Stovall, who used a .45 caliber handgun. McGeorge had represented Stovall's wife in a divorce action, and Stovall apparently was not pleased with the outcome. Stovall was known to be a frequent flyer to the Erie Police Department and had a rap sheet about the size of a roll of toilet paper.

As DiPaolo was assigned to the case, he was informed by an emergency room doctor that two of McGeorge's friends, a detective and an attorney, could be attempting to abscond with two vials of white powder hospital nurses found in McGeorge's shirt pocket. The informing doctor told DiPaolo that as he and a nurse walked into the room, they watched the detective surreptitiously place the vials into his own pocket. At the time of the call from the doctor, DiPaolo had been taking statements from witnesses at police headquarters.

As DiPaolo recalls, this incident with the vials began to overshadow the actual attempted murder, as Mayor Tullio, the police director, city councilmen and the District Attorney were all involved.

While DiPaolo was doing his interviews, Det. Don Dunford, who works in the Identification Section, told DiPaolo that Detective Sergeant William Turner brought McGeorge's clothes from the hospital to be tagged and identified as evidence. Dunford said that Turner showed him two vials and told him not to tag the containers of white powder as it appeared McGeorge would probably die. When Dunford asked whether Turner was assigned to the case, DiPaolo set him straight and said Turner had nothing to do with this investigation. DiPaolo instructed Dunford to immediately send the vials to the Pennsylvania State Police Laboratory to be identified, but to first photograph them, just to make sure they did not disappear. And DiPaolo wanted the photos as proof!

A short time later, Turner and an Erie attorney, not knowing that DiPaolo already knew about the vials and sent them to the state police, told DiPaolo of finding the vials and suggested holding off on having the contents tested until they knew whether McGeorge would make it or not. The attorney said, "Gus is a good guy and this will hurt his family."

DiPaolo was outraged and shouted at Turner to "stay the fuck out of my investigation." He told Turner the vials had already been tagged, and Turner and the attorney left the room. But Police Director Art Berardi summoned DiPaolo from the interrogation room and asked, "What the fuck were you and Turner yelling about?" It should have been obvious as many officers overhead the conversation. But DiPaolo suggested that Berardi that he ask Captain Kangaroo, a nickname given to Turner by another detective years earlier. "He's always sticking his fucking nose in where it doesn't belong," DiPaolo said, telling Berardi to ask Turner why he wanted to keep evidence from being tagged. "He and the lawyer should be arrested!" DiPaolo said.

Many employees at Hamot Medical Center knew what had transpired, as well has half the officers in the Erie Bureau of Police had knowledge that an internal investigation being conducted by Captain Paul DeDionisio Jr. and Lieutenant Dennis Tobin was dragging along slowly. Berardi ordered the investigation.

City Councilmen Mario Bagnoni and Brian Dougherty wanted a Council hearing to determine whether a cover-up was underway. Tullio and Berardi publicly announced there was no "whitewash" of the investigation as piecing together the facts take time. But the Fraternal Order of Police and the Erie Patrolman's Association supported a council hearing.

After two months, and during a news conference, Tullio, Berardi, District Attorney William "Rusty" Cunningham, Captain DeDionisio and Lieutenant Tobin identified Detective Sergeant William Turner as the cop who will receive a five-day suspension for conduct unbecoming an officer. For attempting to confiscate and conceal the vials that contained a substance identified by the Pennsylvania State Police as cocaine, Berardi said the internal investigation by DeDionisio and Tobin turned up no evidence of criminal activity.

Yet DiPaolo, who knew the Pennsylvania Crimes Code inside out, was also aware that tampering with evidence, obstruction of justice and oppression of office, might just have fit this case. But there was no way that was about to happen.

Tullio attempted to justify the suspension as "stiff," but DiPaolo and many others suspected that Turner was Tullio's fair-haired boy, for some unknown reason.

Turner's investigative interview tactics had been common knowledge in the police department, DiPaolo said, often convincing young, uneducated suspects to confess to non-violent crimes they did not commit so Turner would get credit for a high clearance rate, even if others later confessed to the same crimes. "Berardi, DeDionisio and Tobin knew, but did nothing," DiPaolo said.

"Turner was cooking the books before Bernie Madoff knew anything about Ponzi scams," DiPaolo said. "The brass running the detective division knew what he was doing and did nothing with his clearances. The stats made them look good, but they knew they were phony. But by letting them be recorded that way, it fucked up the Uniform Crime Reporting statistics sent to the Feds every year by municipal police departments."

Erie was no different than as any other police department in the United States, DiPaolo believed, with only a very small number of "bad" cops. But the overwhelming majority were good, hard-working, caring and honest men and women who wore their blue uniforms with pride.

DiPaolo explained Turner would get a young suspect who admitted to a retail theft to go for 42 thefts from autos, "even though the kid had nothing to do with them."

Half the Erie County law enforcement community – city, state and Millcreek police – especially the investigators, knew of Turner's M.O. when testifying in court cases, DiPaolo said. "The first story is never the last story. It's called testilying."

DiPaolo said Turner "got a kiss with only a five-day suspension" over the McGeorge incident, but "had the balls to file a grievance." After the grievance procedure hearings were exhausted in Erie, the grievance went before an independent arbitrator from Pittsburgh in 1989.

"As always, Turner gave false testimony, saying the real reason he made the request was because an Identification Section officer didn't appear to know what he was doing," DiPaolo said. But DiPaolo testified that the vials contained cocaine and that Turner knew it would jam up his buddy, McGeorge. The testimony also showed Turner was not involved in the case, even though he indicated to the ID officer that he was, DiPaolo said. "As I said, Turner's first story is never the last story."

The arbitrator, an attorney ruled for the City of Erie, upholding the suspension. But within days of the ruling, Turner was in the hot seat again and disciplined with a letter of reprimand over the personal use of a vehicle he should not have been using.

When Joyce Savocchio became mayor in January of 1990, she had to deal with Turner 30 days later, disciplining him for leaking information to the news media about an ongoing investigation.

"Captain DeDionisio who was now Chief DeDionisio just put up with it," DiPaolo said. "At one point he publicly admitted there were problems in the police bureau. "He was right – there was no leadership," DiPaolo said.

On March 28, 1988, after the lawyer had recovered from his gunshot wounds, DiPaolo swore out an arrest warrant for McGeorge, charging him with possession of cocaine, a controlled substance under the law.

DiPaolo's plan was to wait until the next morning and arrest McGeorge as he entered his office, thinking he might have been in possession of additional amounts of cocaine. DiPaolo later said he "made the mistake of telling Rusty Cunningham, the District Attorney," as Cunningham wanted his chief county detective, Mark Watts, involved in the arrest.

At 6:30 a.m., DiPaolo and Watts set up surveillance near McGeorge's downtown office at West 9th and Peach Streets. At 9 a.m., DiPaolo watched as a WJET-TV news wagon pulled up a block away at 8th and Peach. The cop recognized the camera crew and Reporter Theresa Murtland.

"Who did you tell?" DiPaolo asked Watts. But Watts denied telling anyone. If Watts was being truthful, DiPaolo knew that it was Watts' boss, Cunningham, who had alerted the media.

Leaving Watts in the surveillance car, DiPaolo approached the news van in the midst of the downtown morning rush, and found Murtland in the front passenger seat. "I'm glad to see you're the only news crew here," DiPaolo baited her.

"Oh thanks!" she bit. "Dom, I appreciate it. Rusty told me you would be here to grab Gus." Bingo! DiPaolo had been correct about the leak. Back in the car, DiPaolo told Watts what Murtland had revealed about Cunningham. "I'm not surprised," DiPaolo quoted Watts as saying. Now it was 10 a.m. and no McGeorge. Suddenly, the police radio speaker perked to life as the surveillance team was informed by the Erie police radio operator that McGeorge and his lawyer, Michelle Hawk, were at police headquarters. McGeorge was turning himself in.

To DiPaolo, it was a waste of a morning, but he nonetheless performed his required duties, serving the warrant on McGeorge, having the suspect printed and photographed, and driving him to District Judge Larry Fabrizi's office for arraignment. While DiPaolo did not see lawyer Hawk at police headquarters, she was already at Fabrizi's office, waiting for them to arrive and immediately and loudly confronted DiPaolo.

"This is bullshit," she yelled. "You call the media before you call me, the attorney for Gus?" The tirade lasted several minutes. Eventually, as there were others in his waiting room who were not connected to this case,

Fabrizi said, "Let's keep it down!" But Michelle Hawk continued until DiPaolo said, "Calm down. Take a water pill. You're yelling at the wrong guy. Go talk to Rusty." Soon thereafter, Fabrizi released McGeorge on recognizance bond.

Later, Hawk held a news conference to complain about how the arrest was handled while Cunningham naturally had no comment. At the courthouse, DiPaolo was upset with Cunningham, not because DiPaolo was blamed for the public arrest, but because he and Watts had waited what could have been a productive morning – and DiPaolo blamed Cunningham for that. When DiPaolo confronted Cunningham about it, he first denied it. But when DiPaolo told him that reporter Murtland gave him up, Cunningham said, "You got me!"

DiPaolo thought. It was learned that McGeorge had been tipped off by his secretary that a television van was camped out near his office – so the surveillance and time spent was all for naught.

Stovall, meanwhile, was permitted by his assistant public defender attorney, A.J. Adams, to testify during his trial that McGeorge shot himself, which the jury did not buy and he was convicted and sent to a new home for 20 years. "What a defense! No wonder Tony Logue got rid of Adams as a public defender," DiPaolo said.

But while DiPaolo wanted to learn McGeorge's supplier of the cocaine, Hawk refused to allow her client to speak with the detective as McGeorge and Hawk claimed McGeorge was set-up by DiPaolo. They appeared to be upset with the detective because he would not go along with Turner's plan to ditch the coke.

At that point, Cunningham took over, saying he would personally interview McGeorge. That June, "McGeorge got a kiss just like his pal Turner," DiPaolo said.

He was allowed to plead no-contest for possession of cocaine. Cunningham then approved the plea deal of probation without verdict.

In Judge William Pfadt's chambers, behind closed doors and not in open court in which "regular" criminals are required to appear, and with McGeorge, Hawk, and Cunningham present, McGeorge was sentenced to one year probation. There were no fines or court costs assessed. DiPaolo, the arresting officer, had not been invited to this private session.

Because he reportedly took heat from the law enforcement community, Cunningham made as a condition of the probation McGeorge's requirement to identify his source of the cocaine. He had to give up his supplier. "The media praised Cunningham for making that a requirement as law-abiding citizens supported it. But it was reported that Cunningham never came through with it."

After 33 years, DiPaolo is still waiting for that information.

"So much for fairness and impartiality," DiPaolo said. "So much for credibility and integrity."

CHAPTER 6

JUSTICE FOR JAMES STANLEY AND FRIENDS

On October 4, 1992, James "Shorty" Stanley, 42, was found dead in an Erie alley near West 26th and Peach Streets. DiPaolo, who had just arrived home after Sunday mass, was informed by police headquarters that the chief of police had ordered that he take over the investigation. Detective Gerald McShane, who was on duty at the time, would work the case with DiPaolo.

Within just a few days of working the case with McShane, three men were charged with beating Stanley to death. DiPaolo identified Anthony Paolello, 45, originally from New Jersey and not long in Erie, as the ringleader of the threesome. The others were Anthony DeFranco, 28, and Daniel Funt, 20. All were charged with murder, aggravated assault, robbery and criminal conspiracy in Stanley's death.

Paolello, a convicted felon, was also charged with the rape of a 44-year-old Cleveland woman who was staying in another room at the boarding house where they all were residing. After being attacked, the woman fled to Stanley's and Allen Garfield's room for help, but they were brutally beaten by the three men. While Stanley died, Garfield, 43, remained hospitalized in a coma in intensive care for weeks. The three defendants in the Stanley case were also charged in connection with the Garfield beating.

Because the state parolee DeFranco, who went by "Tone Capone," was thought to have ties to Erie's underworld, the Detectives placed the rape victim and Garfield under protective custody to make sure DeFranco's associates could not get to them. To make sure DeFranco and Paolello could not plot against the witnesses, DiPaolo and McShane had DeFranco transferred to the Warren County Jail, 60 miles away, to await trial.

In April of 1993, the case was ready for trial, but since DiPaolo was a candidate for District Judge and on leave from his police duties, Judge Shad Connelly granted the continuance to the June term as requested by the DA's office.

In the May primary, DiPaolo won both party nominations in a five-man race, virtually assuring he would be elected to office that November.

In late June, Paolello and Funt went on trial. DeFranco's lawyer, William Weichler, was granted his request for a separate trial for his client. According to Garfield's testimony, he and Stanley were in their apartment when Marlene Valentta appeared at their door, half naked with ripped clothing and bleeding from her head. As Stanley was about to call the police, Garfield testified, the three suspects rushed into the apartment and beat them. Garfield awoke several weeks later in the hospital intensive care unit with twenty-two broken ribs. He then learned that his friend Stanley was dead. Valentta testified about the rape and the beating by the men.

On July 2, following four days of trial and six hours of jury deliberations, DiPaolo heard "the most satisfying word a Detective can ever hear in any criminal case – 'Guilty.'"

Said DiPaolo, "It's difficult to describe the emotion one feels after taking a case from Day One, doing all you can for the victims, and then hearing the verdict in open court." DiPaolo had 185 jury trials in his career, hearing the word "guilty" in 183 of them.

The ringleader Paolello, as the "prime actor" and "principle mover," was found guilty of first degree murder. The jury found Funt guilty of third degree murder, which DiPaolo believed was justified for Funt's actions as compared with Paolello's and DeFranco's. When the penalty phase of the trial followed, the jury was unanimous in its decision to sentence Paolello to death instead of life in prison without parole. Judge Shad Connelly formally sentenced Paolello to death by lethal injection, and also 12-to-25 years on charges related to Valentta and Garfield. It marked the first Erie County death penalty sentence since 1978.

Funt, meanwhile, was sentenced in August to serve 27½ to 55 years in prison. Connelly told Funt there was little doubt of his involvement, as he had no guts while wearing a mask to hide himself during the crimes, as well as showing no remorse.

Funt had had some minor scrapes with the law, but Paolello had 19 prior convictions, including three federal felony charges.

Prior to DeFranco's trial, "Tone Capone" was offered a plea deal in the wake of what happened to the other two. He would plead guilty to third degree murder, the other charges would be dropped, he would be sentenced to 10 to 20 years in prison, but with no objection to an early parole. Attorney Weichler, however, who was paid by DeFranco's father and uncle, refused the offer, saying the cops did not have enough evidence for conviction. "Tone Capone rolled the dice and got snake eyes," DiPaolo said. It took the jury only four hours before DiPaolo heard the magic word again: Guilty! Guilty of second degree murder and life without parole. When Connelly sentenced him, the judge mocked him for being "a real tough guy beating helpless men." When the death penalty case against Paolello was automatically appealed, the first degree murder conviction was upheld, but the actual death penalty was vacated by the Pennsylvania Supreme Court on the lack of aggravating circumstances needed for such a penalty. Aggravating circumstances must outweigh mitigating circumstances. But since there was only one of each, the court tossed the death penalty and converted the sentence to life without the possibility of parole.

DeFranco's and Paolello's appeals were also denied, and both got life without parole, and, as Paulie Walnuts on The Sopranos says when one of the boys got life, "He got from now on." It is also known the only way a lifer gets parole is called a "Back Door Parole", when they die and the Coroner wheels them out the back door of the prison. DiPaolo has had a few of them, B.D.P.

For DiPaolo, it was the 32nd and last murder case in a 25-year police career. Five months later, DiPaolo became a District Judge. While all homicide investigations are important, DiPaolo and McShane had explained to ADA Jim Vogel, the prosecutor, that this one was of particular importance. Stanley, Garfield and Valennta had nobody in their lives. No family. No friends. None were from Erie.

At one time, they were productive citizens from Texas, Michigan and Ohio. They were fathers; Valennta a mother. But for various reasons they left their families and jobs and turned to alcohol, living day to day on the streets, city to city, flop houses to railroad cars to parks and vacant buildings. It was truly skid row to them. No family holidays and birthdays with their kids. As such, they were vulnerable to the criminal elements. "Regardless of who they were, or where they came from and how they lived, they did not deserve to be beaten, which resulted in Stanley's death," DiPaolo said.

CHAPTER 7

THE COP DiPAOLO AND "BIG LOU" THE MAYOR

By early 1981, Erie City Councilman Mario Bagnoni, the former Detective Deputy Chief of the Erie Bureau of Police, an outspoken man who frequently butted heads with and criticized Mayor Louis Tullio, made the decision to oppose "Big Lou" in the spring Democratic Party mayoral primary election.

DiPaolo, meanwhile, had held the powerful political position of Sixth Ward Democratic Party Chairman; the Sixth was one of Erie's largest Ward and the home of many local elected officials. A year earlier, he had been the only county Ward Chairman to openly endorse Democrat Michael Veshecco, in 1979, a young assistant Erie County District Attorney, who was running against his boss, the incumbent Democrat Robert Chase in the open primary election. Many of the older Democratic Party guard thought DiPaolo was committing political suicide by convincing his 34-person ward committee to go along with his endorsement. But Veshecco handily won the Democratic primary, and on so-doing boosted DiPaolo's political standing a capital in the community.

Now, when Bagnoni decided to run in 1981, he wanted DiPaolo to become involved in his campaign, but not openly, saying, "You know how Tullio is. He'll hold it against you."

"Look" DiPaolo said, "even though I'm a Detective, I'm still receiving Patrolman's pay. So what can Big Lou do? Make me walk a beat? I'm for you, Bags, and not hiding it!"

As a result, DiPaolo became Bagnoni's Erie westside coordinator. The leadership of the Bagnoni campaign team included Gene "Jeep" Placidi as the overall chair, Edward Sparaga, a respected businessman, Erie School Director, and member of the local Polish-American community, as the eastside coordinator. That was the year Tullio raised $70,000, an awesome amount for a primary race, while Bagnoni raised only $11,000. Bags would have raised much more, DiPaolo believes, but he often sent back donations to those he believed could not afford to spend their money on a political campaign. Bagnoni would often say, "Her husband just died, or, the family has a lot of kids, or, he was laid off from work."

While DiPaolo attempted to convince Bagnoni that the campaign committee needed the funds to compete with Tullio, Bags refused to hear it, saying, "I'm the candidate and it's my call."

"That's the kind of man Bags was," DiPaolo would later say.

DiPaolo recalled that his father, Pat DiPaolo, had been heavily involved in local Democratic Party politics for many years, dating back to the Mike Cannavino days of the 1950s and 1960s. One day, Al Ferraro, owner of a Ford dealership, phoned Pat. Ferraro, a Tullio supporter, asked Pat to join him for lunch as he had a message from Tullio. The message? Tullio was disappointed that Dom was in Bagnoni's camp. But if Dom would withdraw as westside coordinator, stay out of the race, not endorse Bagnoni and convince his Sixth Warders to avoid helping Bags, then Tullio would promote DiPaolo to lieutenant after the primary election, and then make him a captain at the start of the year. Pat told Ferraro he doesn't tell his son what to do, but would pass along the information.

When father and son talked, they laughed about the offer, not believing that Tullio was being truthful, but also thinking that Dom would go back on his word.

"I'm committed to Bagnoni and would never go back on my promise," Dom told Pat. "Don't even call Ferraro back. He'll get the hint."

About two weeks later, Danny Savocchio and Hector DiTullio, both Pat's longtime friends and Tullio supporters, visited Pat at his home. They told Pat that the mayor wanted very much to promote Dominick, but could not do so with Dom openly working against him in the election.

The deal got even better: First lieutenant, then captain, and in two years, deputy chief of detectives! According to what the two men told Pat, Tullio believed Dom was one of the best detectives on the force, but Tullio does not agree with DiPaolo's politics. Pat again said he would pass along the information to his son.

When that happened, they both cracked up again, with Dom joking, "Maybe the next time the offer with be Chief of Police or even assistant to the mayor!" When the dust finally settled from the primary election, Tullio had defeated Mario Bagnoni, a difference of about 1,000 votes. After that, life went on for DiPaolo, who had no second-thoughts about his helping Bagnoni.

"Bagnoni had been an honest cop, politician and dedicated family man, and I had the utmost respect for him," DiPaolo later said.

On February 5, 1982, less than two months into Tullio's new four-year term of office, he promoted 47 police officers through the bureau, including 20 detectives of the 23 in the division. DiPaolo, his partner, D.C. Gunter, and Hank Aldrete, were the only detectives not promoted.

While many deserved to be promoted, DiPaolo said, some were also "Tullio's boys who got rewarded for helping him, for purchasing tickets for his fundraisers, and, as such, received political paybacks."

One promotion in particular irritated DiPaolo.

"Frank Rotunda, who would not know enough to come out of the rain, was later convicted of solicitation of murder, dealing cocaine and participating in home invasions and was sentenced to 10 years in prison, was one of big Lou's confidants." You don't run with the cops, and root for the robbers, DiPaolo would say.

Just nine days later, on February 14, Detective DiPaolo was honored by the Erie Jaycees as Policeman of the Year, and was later selected as First Runner-up for the state Jaycees' Pennsylvania Policeman of the Year. Out of 50 state regions (50 police officers), DiPaolo was ranked second in the state based on performance and dedication to his community.

In early December 1982, WSEE-TV investigative reporter Carol Pella asked to interview DiPaolo for an investigative piece she was doing on police promotions. She wanted to know how someone could be named local Policeman of the Year and state runner-up for the same honor, yet get passed over for promotion. She said everyone knew the reason was that DiPaolo did not support Tullio.

DiPaolo declined the interview, thanking Pella for her support, but said he preferred not to get into that kind of public criticism and was only interested in doing his job.

DiPaolo knew that Tullio had a system that involved cops and city employees purchasing tickets to the mayor's political fundraisers. Those who bought tickets, DiPaolo said, received four hours of overtime pay.

"That's why he would pack his parties," DiPaolo said. "He should have gone to jail as he was the master of macing!" Macing is the illegal act of politicians forcing public servants to contribute to their campaigns.

Several detectives urged DiPaolo to purchase the tickets just to get the overtime pay. He would not have to attend the parties. "No thanks!" DiPaolo would answer.

On one occasion, Deputy Chief John Cousins asked DiPaolo, "Doesn't your family need the extra money?"

"That's why I work two jobs," DiPaolo answered.

But on December 21, while on the street and working a rape case, DiPaolo received a radio transmission ordered him to immediately contact Chief of Police Richard Skonieczka. "Now what did I do?" DiPaolo thought? "Pinch some politicians family member or buddy?"

When DiPaolo spoke by phone with the Chief, also known by his friends as "Skinny," the chief was laughing. "Are you sitting down?" he said. "I got a call from Pat Liebel."

"And?" DiPaolo asked, knowing Liebel was Tullio's longtime administrative assistant.

"She told me to be in the mayor's office with you at 9 a.m. tomorrow. She also said you can bring your wife, kids and parents as the mayor is going to promote you!"

DiPaolo, thinking Skinny was trying to pull some kind of a pre-holiday joke, as it was only a few days before Christmas of 1982, said, "Okay, what do you really want? I'm in the middle a rape investigation."

"I'm serious, Dom!" "I am as surprised as you are!"

Skinny and DiPaolo had been friends away from work as well, playing ball together, and going out to dinner with their wives. Janet DiPaolo and Marilyn Skonieczka were also friends, as many cops' wives became close. The couples had been having dinner together at Fredrico's Port of Call the night before Skonieczka was named chief. Often, Skinny would tell DiPaolo, "I wish there was something I could do for you – but you know him." The reference, DiPaolo knew, was to Tullio.

Now, Skonieczka was saying, "I'm not kidding or lying to you. I wouldn't do that. I don't know what happened, but just be there and bring Janet and your family." That night, Marilyn Skonieczka phoned Janet to say how happy she was for the family as the promotion was long overdue. That night at 9 o'clock, Skonieczka himself phoned DiPaolo to say he had just spoken with the mayor, who wanted to make sure DiPaolo would be present in his office the next morning. "Be in my office at 8:30 a.m.," Skinny said, "and we'll go up to the mayor's office on the fifth flood together."

The next day, Wednesday, December 22, 1982, Dom and Janet arrived at City Hall on time. Pat and Dawn (their children) had school, it being the last day before the holiday break, and DiPaolo's parents declined as the senior Pat DiPaolo indicated a reluctance to be in the same room as Tullio.

When the chief and the DiPaolos walked into Room 511, adjacent to the mayor's office, the media was already there – many of Erie's newspaper, radio and television reporters. It was Tullio's practice, in those days, to hold Thursday press conferences to announce newsworthy items and also to keep his name constantly before the public.

WSEE-TV reporter Carol Pella immediately approached the DiPaolos, hugging each and whispering to Dom, "He is finally doing the right thing. I'll talk with you later, but not here!"

Tullio arrived and the news conference began with DiPaolo realizing he was the only cop being promoted that day. Tullio told the group that DiPaolo had been a detective for 12 of his 13 years with the bureau, and was one of the original members of the Erie Metro Drug Unit working undercover in the early 1970s. He then was assigned to the Narcotics and Intelligence Unit, and later as the youngest Detective in C.I.D. (Criminal Investigation Division). The mayor went on the say he was promoting DiPaolo for his "outstanding record and on the recommendations of Chief Skonieczka and DiPaolo's superiors," adding that DiPaolo earned high ratings during a recent bureau evaluation and had been named "Police Office of the Year" by the Erie and Pennsylvania Jaycees.

Presenting DiPaolo with a Detective-Sergeant gold shield and stripes for his Dress Blues uniform, he shook hands with the DiPaolos and announced he was leaving for a month-long California vacation and would not be back before late January.

Later Skonieczka pulled DiPaolo aside to say that Tullio told him he would announce that Skonieczka recommended him. "Hey, you got the boost in pay – so what?"

"Believe me, I knew nothing about this until I got the call from Liebel," Skonieczka said. "But something prompted him to call a news conference for just one promotion." DiPaolo believed the chief. He also learned the reason for the quick promotion.

That night, reporter Pella phoned DiPaolo at home to say that just two days earlier, on Tuesday, December 20, she had told Tullio that "everyone in Erie knows that Dom DiPaolo is the best and hardest working detective you have and the only reason he's not promoted is that he backed Mario Bagnoni – you promoted everyone but him, and to make it look good, you stuck it to his partner Gunter (who moved to Florida a year later)." Pella told Tullio she was going to do a story about it, but DiPaolo did not want to be interviewed.

"But after he was honored as the cop of the year, I'm going to do it without him as this isn't right." Tullio responded that the Bagnoni support was not the reason for the lack of a promotion and told Pella to leave his office.

Only four Policemen at the time had their Masters Degree in Criminology in the Erie Police Department. Three of them over the years went through the ranks with promotions by the Mayor. One was a Patrolman his entire career, that was David Bagnoni, Mario's son. DiPaolo said, "Do you think Tullio told Pella the truth?" In that, he didn't hold it against anyone that supported Bagnoni.

"I was shocked on Wednesday afternoon when we got a call from Pat Liebel about the news conference!" Pella said.

DiPaolo often said that if it wasn't for Pella, he would have spent his entire police career as a patrolman.

A short time later and after Tullio returned from California, while DiPaolo was working a homicide case, he was told by police Captain Walter Tofel to meet Tullio in the second floor conference room at the downtown Avalon Hotel. When DiPaolo protested, saying he needed to be on the case, Tofel assured him the meeting would be short.

DiPaolo could not imagine what Tullio was up to as they had not spoken since the press conference.

But in the hotel conference room, he was met by Tullio, his assistant, Joe Gardocki, Erie County Democratic Party Chairman Paul Foust, Erie City Councilman Joe Walzack, and Bob Casey, who would be making his fourth run for governor in Pennsylvania in several years, and obviously supported by Tullio. Although Casey was from Scranton on the other side of the state, both he and Tullio were Holy Cross alums.

"I know you're busy," Tullio said, "but I wanted you to meet Bob Casey." He told Casey that DiPaolo was the Sixth Ward Chairman, a good detective, and would help Casey with his election bid.

"He is a good friend of ours," Tullio said, wrongfully indicating that DiPaolo was now one of the boys.

DiPaolo was polite and left, thinking, "This guy Tullio is fucking nuts. How did he know I would be for Casey." But DiPaolo was already backing Casey anyway.

Months later, as DiPaolo was exiting the elevator in the city hall basement to retrieve his detective car, he ran into Tullio. "Just the guy I want to see," Tullio said. "You know that Roger Fischer and Dick Nygaard are running for judge and I want you to support them."

"I'm on Roger's committee," DiPaolo said. "But Nygaard is a Republican and I can't support him."

"Hey," Tullio said, raising his voice, "he's a good friend of mine!"

"Fine," DiPaolo said. "But he's a Republican."

"Did you forget I helped you out?" Tullio asked. "Now you refuse to help me?"

"Mayor, I don't support or vote for Republicans. I'm a Democratic ward chairman. If this promotion was all about helping out with your friends, you can have the gold shield and stripes back."

Tullio could only stare at DiPaolo. The mayor got into the elevator, and that was the last time the two of them ever spoke to one another, which DiPaolo was fine with.

In 1984, Tullio hired Art Berardi as Director of Police Operations, a title akin to commission in other cities.

"This guy was a bigger asshole than Tullio," DiPaolo thought. "He would tell the troops that if they were loyal to him and Tullio, they would all get along fine. He was a blow bag and had a lot of baggage."

By 1985, with Tullio running for his sixth four-year term, there were many in the community who wanted to see a Tullio-Bagnoni rematch. Although Mario did not want to run for mayor again, he entered the fray after learning that no one else would.

But soon it was learned that City Controller Chris Maras might be interested in running for mayor. Bagnoni told Maras he would drop out and support Maras, urge Bagnoni's committee to support him and endorse him himself, according to DiPaolo. He told Maras that three candidates in the race would ensure Tullio another term. But Maras declined the offer. He told Bags he did not want to run.

On the last day to file nominating petitions, Maras jumped into the race, as rumors flew that it was Tullio who put Maras there to make sure Bagnoni would not win. Maras gave up his controller's position to run as his term wasn't up. "Supposedly, he was promised a big job by Big Lou, a job in state government, for his help, as everyone knew Maras could not win," DiPaolo said.

Even though DiPaolo knew it was nearly impossible to now defeat Tullio "with Maras now in it, I became Bagnoni's westside coordinator. I had to do it for Bags."

The Democratic primary election results for mayor showed Tullio won, defeating Bagnoni by less than two thousand votes, with Maras coming in third with more than fifty five hundred votes.

"Be the judge and do the math," DiPaolo said. "Without Maras in the race, Tullio would have been gone."

With Tullio fuming that DiPaolo had been against him again, the Police Director came out with what was known as "The DiPaolo Rule." It said that no Erie police officer could be affiliated with any political party as a committee person. It was effective immediately. There had been a handful of officers who serve as Democratic Party Committeemen, and DiPaolo, of course, was a Ward Chairman.

The rule meant that after 16 years as a committeeman and 14 years as ward chair, DiPaolo was forced to resign the party positions. While Bagnoni and others urged DiPaolo to fight the action, DiPaolo said that while he enjoyed politics, at least he could now spend more time with his family. But the move, while not hurting DiPaolo as Tullio had intended, served to provide Bagnoni with another motive for fighting Tullio and Berardi.

Finally, in late 1988, Bagnoni got the support of other city council members to remove the funding for Berardi from the 1989 City of Erie budget.

"He is milking the taxpayers as he does not do anything," Bagnoni said.

But prior to the council vote, Berardi resigned.

"Now, from 1985 until 1989, Chris Maras had no job," DiPaolo said. "Big Lou fucked him as he never got Maras a job with the state like he promised. Everybody in politics knew Tullio used Maras, including the two statues in Perry Square Park across from City Hall."

By 1989, Maras ran for and won the office of Erie City Treasurer. The longtime city treasurer, Carl "Skip" Cannavino, had given up the job to run for mayor that year in a crowded field. But even though Maras won, he could not find an insurance company to bond him.

"With all the millions of dollars the treasurer is charged with collecting, including all of the real estate or property taxes, officials must be bonded or insured to protect the public's money," DiPaolo explained. "But he could not be insured and still had no job. Karma is a bitch for what he did to Bags."

Skip Cannavino, who had been city treasurer for 32 years, was now running for mayor. He was the nephew of Mike Cannavino, who had initially defeated Tullio in the 1965 Democratic mayoral primary. But Mike Cannavino, a longtime city councilman, unexpectedly died less than two weeks before the November election. The Democratic committee members then chose Tullio to run against the first-term Republican incumbent Charles Williamson, and with the win, that's how Tullio's mayoral legacy began.

Skip Cannavino, in a strange twist of fate, was also Tullio's nephew! Skip's dad was Mike's brother, while Skip's mom was Tullio's sister. While Skip got along with Uncle Lou most of the time, there was always some animosity from Tullio that Skip had supported his uncle Mike and not Uncle Lou in 1965.

"Lou used to say the animosity was over, but you're dealing with someone who thought he was the king," DiPaolo said. Not only was Skip Cannavino in the seven-candidate mayoral race in 1989, but the other candidates were as well-known as Skip. One, Tullio's longtime assistant Patricia Liebel, was seeking the top job with her boss' blessing. But when polling showed it was unlikely for Liebel to win, Tullio shifted his support.

DiPaolo would laugh as he said that many cops, including the brass, wore Liebel buttons and had Liebel bumper stickers on their cars. "But all of a sudden, one day they were all for Joyce Savocchio, a city councilwoman whom Tullio controlled."

Skip Cannavino, who would never be supported by his uncle, lost to Savocchio and after 24 years of Tullio rule at Erie City Hall, DiPaolo believed that nothing had changed.

"All city departments and their Bureau Chiefs stayed the same, including the police. The picnic continued for the chief and all his brass. The incompetence of leadership continued," DiPaolo said.

For DiPaolo, the light at the end of the tunnel came several years later with his retirement.

"I loved my job. I loved solving crimes, but for me it was time for the back-stabbing political bullshit to be over with," he said.

CHAPTER 8

AN HONORABLE QUARTER-CENTURY IN LAW ENFORCEMENT; RISING TO THE NEXT LEVEL

DiPaolo's 25-year law enforcement career – which would culminate with Erie City Council honoring him as the 200-year-old city's most decorated police officer ever, took a number of twists and turns through the rocky paths of Erie's eastside and westside mean streets.

A tough cop, who took a great and often personal interest in each of his cases – from garage break-ins to mass murders – DiPaolo became Erie's lead homicide investigator during the time spanning parts of the 1970s through the early-1990s. During more than two decades, DiPaolo investigated 32 homicides. Of those, many defendants are still doing life terms without parole.

Of his more than 2,000 arrests, only 185 chose to risk jury trials, and only two were found not guilty – a jaw-dropping conviction rate by every standard of measurement. The others all settled for pleas or other agreements. In 1973, DiPaolo was honored by local and Pennsylvania Jaycees for making 231 felony arrests out for the 274 made by the entire Erie Bureau of Police.

The thoroughness of his investigations, thus, saved Erie City and Erie County taxpayers untold thousands of dollars in would-be court costs had so many of his cases gone to jury trials. Over the years, DiPaolo's career achievements were repeatedly recognized by the local news media, particularly the local newspapers in recounting not only his accomplishments, but awards by colleges and universities, the Erie County Bar Association, businesses and police organizations.

His most renowned and widely reported-upon investigations involved the mass murder of a family of five, including three children, by the childrens' own father; the mob-related hit of a well-known Erie bookie; the murder of an Erie police officer; million-dollar burglaries, and arsons.

As an integral member of the prosecution team, DiPaolo went up against nationally-renowned defense attorneys, former U.S. Attorney General Ramsey Clark, and even the storied former New York City cop, Frank Serpico.

In addition to the routine thugs that plague most of the country's urban areas, DiPaolo never differentiated between the rich and famous and those others. If they did the crime, he believed, they must do the time. As such, the rich and famous had no excuses, DiPaolo believed, and in many ways were worse than the low-lives he dealt with on a daily basis. He arrested attorneys, physicians, teachers, a police chief, cops, nurses, politicians, and even wealthy mobsters. He never picked and chose between who he sent to jail. Regardless of who they were, or their status in life, if they broke the law, they were arrested.

Not surprisingly, during a mob-hit investigation, the players put out a contract on DiPaolo's life. But it was called off when DiPaolo's former partner, Detective David Bagnoni, son of the popular Erie City Councilman Mario Bagnoni, got wind of the plot. Pennsylvania state police confirmed the planned hit when one of the co-conspirators was wire-tapped.

DiPaolo particularly loathed Italian-Americans who chose to cross the line. Proud of his and his family's ethnic heritage, woe be to Italian-Americans who found themselves on the wrong side of DiPaolo's investigations. Too many honest Italians had worked too long and too hard to have their reputations tainted by a crooked few.

All the while through his police career, DiPaolo and his wife, Janet, were deeply involved with their church, chairing or co-chairing many committees and activities.

DiPaolo immersed himself in youth activities, becoming athletic director at a Catholic grade school, his alma mater, Sacred Heart, coaching football and basketball, while at the same time Janet coached cheerleading. In 24 years, they made innumerable friends for life.

Patrick, their son, played and starred in three sports in high school, and then in college. Later, he became the assistant coach of baseball at Thiel College, his alma mater in Greenville, Pa., before returning to Erie to coach football at his high school, Cathedral Preparatory School, and at Central High School.

At 33, he became an assistant principal, then principal in the Erie School District, and was considered one of the district's top administrators when he was struck down with Lyme Disease. Patrick fought this insidious illness for 63 months until it finally claimed him at age 44. He left a wife, Beth, and two beautiful young children, Julia and Dominick ("Nico"). A community-wide scholarship was founded in Pat's name, resulting in thousands of dollars being raised and contributed to dozens of Erie County student/athletes.

The DiPaolos' daughter, Dawn Marie, also excelled in sports in high school and was an Erie dancer for many years, participating in a number of dance reviews. After graduating from Gannon University, she was employed by a local law firm before becoming manager for her dad's magisterial district office for over 24 years. Dawn, currently administrative assistant to the superintendent of the Edmond L. Thomas Juvenile Detention Center, is married to Michael Romeo; they are the parents of two beautiful children, Gino and Gianna.

As a result of all this, the DiPaolo family was well-recognized and respected, not only in "Little Italy" and the Sixth Ward, but throughout the Erie community and beyond. DiPaolo had achieved a statewide reputation in law enforcement, a reputation he would soon parlay into continued public service.

Toward the end of DiPaolo's police career, he became a training officer for young officers who wanted to become detectives. This, DiPaolo welcomed, as it was an opportunity to help educate young officers on proper investigative procedures and protocol, including investigative techniques, writing search warrants and criminal complaints, and collecting and tagging evidence, all to make sure their work was done according to Hoyle and would not get suppressed during trials and lead to losing cases and further hurting victims. One such new trainee was Frank Kwitowski, whom DiPaolo was both pleased and proud of his progress and adaption to becoming an investigator. Kwitowski was later promoted through the ranks, ultimately becoming the captain in charge of the detective division.

DiPaolo's last trainee was a young African-American officer with a "party guy" reputation in the patrol division. After two months with the officer, DiPaolo was asked by a superior officer how the young trainee was doing. "Very well," DiPaolo responded. "He caught on pretty fast; I even let him do our last investigation on his own."

But the Detective Lieutenant replied, "Well, you know he is a little of a loose cannon, but we had to take him although we really don't want him in the division, if you know what I mean."

"Well, why was he assigned to the training program if you didn't want him here?" DiPaolo asked. "Because he is a loose cannon or because he is black."

"I just wanted you to know our feelings before you do your evaluation," the lieutenant said. "Don't get crazy with it."

But DiPaolo graded the trainee as outstanding in all four categories of the evaluation. As a result, the officer had to be kept in the detective division. If the brass had tried to keep him out, DiPaolo would have gone straight to the F.O.P. to file a complaint that would include his conversation with the lieutenant.

DiPaolo warned the young officer to "watch his ass," as he did with all trainees, but never told him the real reason. The new detective turned out to be proficient in the division, but DiPaolo's training days were over, as he refused to become involved with further "cronyism" that existed for whatever reason his career ended.

CHAPTER 9

THE '90s: FROM COPPER BLUE TO JUDICIAL ROBES; AN EASY TRANSITION

By 1993, the veteran cop DiPaolo was not only ready, but prepared to use his decades-long political experience at the next level of the criminal justice system. Taking a deep breath, and with the approval of his family, he tossed his hat into the political arena for the first time and ran for District Justice in Erie's sprawling Sixth Ward. He had five opponents in that first race, including the incumbent, but he won in a landslide. Dominick DiPaolo, the tough cop, was now the TOUGH – BUT FAIR – JUDGE.

As judicial races are considered politically non-partisan, DiPaolo had assured himself victory being the only candidate listed on both Democratic and Republican ballots in the November 1993 general election. As there were no viable write-in candidates, he easily won.

Later in November, he attended the mandatory four-week Pennsylvania minor-judiciary school for new District Justices at Wilson College in Chambersburg. Between the hundreds of hours of vacation time and accumulated compensatory time, DiPaolo was about to attend the school while he expected to be paid and also take off the remainder of the year. But it did not turn out that way. In those pre-cell phone and pre-automatic paycheck deposit days, DiPaolo's friend and ex-partner David Bagnoni, who DiPaolo had arranged to pick-up his bi-weekly paychecks and deliver to Janet for deposit, phoned DiPaolo's Chambersburg motel with alarming news: No paycheck!

Bagnoni told DiPaolo that then Chief DeDionisio claimed that DiPaolo had retired.

"I know we never saw eye-to-eye," DiPaolo said of DeDionisio, "but this was a low blow, obviously to hurt my family, not me."

DiPaolo immediately checked with Fraternal Order of Police President Ted Marnen, who confirmed no retirement papers had been filed, and spoke with Attorney Donald Wright, a good friend of Mayor Joyce Savocchio's. Both Marnen and Wright promised to immediately look into the matter.

Wright got back to DiPaolo, he said, alleging that DeDionisio told Savocchio DiPaolo retired immediately after the election. When Wright asked Savocchio about the retirement paperwork DiPaolo was required to sign, she told him DeDionisio had it, but was off that day.

"As always, she was no help, but it was another case of her getting the wool pulled over her eyes. The job was over her head," DiPaolo said.

According to DiPaolo, DeDionisio insisted DiPaolo had to retire after winning the general election because he was now a District Justice and could no longer be a cop. "But what this rocket scientist did not realize was that my term did not begin until I was first certified by the state after passing the test from the minor judiciary school on December 5, 1993, but more importantly, that I could not be sworn in as the Sixth Ward District Justice until January 3, 1994," DiPaolo said.

Attorney Wright, F.O.P. President Marnen, F.O.P. Attorney Chuck Agresti, and even City Councilman Mario Bagnoni all attempted to explain to Savocchio and DeDionisio that a city employee cannot be retired without them knowing it or signing off on the proper forms.

"It was unbelievable to me that Savocchio went along with DeDionsio's vindictive plan to try to stick it to me on the way out the door." So, after 25 years of exemplary service to the City of Erie, a spotless record, never being suspended from duty, being honored by city council as the most decorated cop ever in Erie, DiPaolo threatened to file a lawsuit in federal court over the salary he was due and his earned pension. And he was going to go public with it. But he first had to file a grievance through the Fraternal Order of Police, in that order.

Six months after DiPaolo left the police bureau and was a District Justice, and after discussions between Attorney Charles Agresti and city officials, DiPaolo withdrew his grievance and the City of Erie gave him back-pay from November and December 1993 and early 1994, along with his full pension. His retirement was effective January 3, 1994.

DiPaolo believes that DeDionisio's motive had been an attempt to prevent DiPaolo from staying on the force to January 1, 1994, when he, along with all the other officers, was entitled to a four percent raise. The raise would increase DiPaolo's pension by several dollars. "Talk about being vindictive and jealous," DiPaolo later said.

But what pissed off DiPaolo even more was that while the retirement issue festered, Savocchio sent him a letter of congratulations on his election victory. "No clue whatsoever," he said of her.

DiPaolo was also remembering in August 1989, two months after Savocchio won the Mayor's race as she was assured taking office in January 1990, that DiPaolo received a call from his good friend Attorney Don Wright who was very close to Savocchio over the years and was a big supporter.

Wright knowing DiPaolo supported Skip Cannavino for Mayor asked if he would be willing to sit down with Savocchio and give her some direction with the Police Department, as she was getting a lot of stories on how it was being run, or should be run..

DiPaolo thought about it and figured maybe Savocchio would take some of his ideas which would make the Department better for everyone. He met with her off duty at the Knox Law Firm for more than four hours going through each Division in the Department. She appeared to be very receptive and they met two more times, with DiPaolo giving her a Chain of Command Structure and the amount of Officers that should be in each Division.

Wright advised DiPaolo she was very appreciative for what DiPaolo did for her.

In January 1990, she took office and nothing changed and the morale got worse. And the incompetence continued which was bad for the young guys as they were not being taught the right way.

When it was over, DiPaolo said, "Talk about dysfunctional incompetence in city government, all on the taxpayers' dime! I wasn't surprised at what DeDionisio tried to pull off, but to think that Savocchio knowingly went along with something so illegal and wrong showed she was no better than Big Lou. Cronyism at its worst."

But, as judge, DiPaolo lived by that motto, tough but fair, practicing what he preached every day on the job.

By 1996, his excellent relationship with the local media continued as DiPaolo again made headlines for acts above and beyond his judicial duties. An armed man had taken hostages and barricaded himself inside a home. Police attempted without success to negotiate with the hostage-taker, futilely trying to talk him out of the potentially deadly situation. The suspect, who DiPaolo had arrested many years earlier, finally agreed to surrender. But only to DiPaolo.

Police advised the suspect that DiPaolo was no longer a cop. The gunman knew that, he told the cops. Hell, he said, he even voted for the judge. But would talk with and give up only to DiPaolo. At that very moment, DiPaolo was home having dinner with his family. The police captain who reluctantly phoned the judge at home explained the situation. He offered to lie to the gunman, saying the cops could not locate DiPaolo. But the judge, upon hearing the suspect's name did not hesitate.

Immediately heading to the scene, he entered the home alone and after only a few minutes convinced the suspect, armed with a high-powered rifle, to surrender. It was a happy ending for all: The cops. The gunman. And especially for the hostages. And the media praised DiPaolo for his selfless actions.

There was no doubt the positive and extensive media exposure DiPaolo received during his 25 years in law enforcement and also as the Democratic

Party's Sixth Ward Chairman for 14 years helped him get elected in his home ward. In one of his first official actions in office, DiPaolo formed a group of Sixth Ward citizens to create a volunteer Juvenile Diversion Committee. This group would address juvenile offenders the very first time they became involved in the criminal justice system, DiPaolo's aim being to help those kids get back on the straight and narrow before they had a chance to become career criminals, and hopefully for good.

By this time, DiPaolo was one of the most-recognized public servants in Erie County. The positive media attention which he achieved as a police officer, plus his reputation for fairness, followed him and continued through his judicial career.

CHAPTER 10

ELECTION LOW-LIGHTS OF 1993

In 1993, Tom Carney was living in the Sixth Ward, and now, after the death of longtime District Judge Larry Fabrizi and with help of Carney's longtime friend, John Vendetti, a District Judge in the Third Ward, Carney jumped into the race in the Sixth Ward.

DiPaolo was also in that same 1993 race, along with Robbie Fabrizi, Larry's son, and two other candidates. Larry had died the previous October, with the election set for May of 1993, some seven months later. While there had been some talk that there might be a gubernatorial appointment to fill the seat, Erie County President Judge Jess Jiuliante quickly brought an end to such speculation by advising all the candidates there would be no appointment – none would get the nod or advantage over another and all five candidates were on their own.

But apparently this did not sit well with Carney and his political pal at the time, then State Senator Anthony "Buzz" Andrezeski. In March of 1993, just two months before the primary election, Carney, who had worked at Erie's Hammermill Paper Company and was involved with the union there, was appointed by Governor Robert Casey a Democrat, to fill Fabrizi's unexpired term. DiPaolo learned that Andrezeski convinced Casey to appoint Carney to the position (saying Carney has a doctorate in people skills and would be outstanding, which flabbergasted DiPaolo, and many more) pending the outcome of the upcoming primary and general elections. Meanwhile, Juiliante was livid. The election was held on schedule, and DiPaolo won, with Fabrizi finishing in second place and Carney in third place. DiPaolo defeated Carney by more than 2,500 votes. But Carney was to remain in office until that December, as DiPaolo could not be seated on the bench until January 1994.

"Unfortunately, for the citizens of the Sixth Ward of Erie, and members of the legal profession, Carney had no idea what he was doing," DiPaolo later mused.

For example, the day after the May 1993 primary election, Carney presided over a murder hearing involving a young woman charged with stabbing her boyfriend to death. Carney became judge and jury at the conclusion of the hearing, ruling that Patricia Foster had acted in self-defense and was not guilty of the crime. As a result, she was released from the Erie County Jail.

"This is what happens when politicians – state senators and even governors – get involved in the judicial system with political appointments," DiPaolo said.

The Erie County District Attorney's office re-filed the criminal complaints before another District Justice, and all charges were bound over to court, resulted in Foster later pleading guilty and going to prison.

Meanwhile, Jiuliante phoned DiPaolo and asked if he was willing to start his term early. Jiuliante indicated to DiPaolo that Carney was in over his head and was considering having him removed from office.

But still a Detective Sergeant, DiPaolo was involved in his last homicide investigation and besides, he was scheduled to attend a special school to certify incoming District Judges. So, he could not step in before January. Fabrizi's secretary, his sister, Elaine Hill, retired as soon as Carney took over. Jiuliante told DiPaolo that Carney was going to hire a secretary, but the judge instructed Carney to hire the woman DiPaolo planned to hire, his daughter, Dawn DiPaolo-Romeo, as she would stay in the office. Carney complied with the order.

DiPaolo considered the next seven months disasters in the Sixth Ward's Judicial District. But the following January, DiPaolo was swept into office, and Carney went back to the Hammermill Paper Company.

The first thing DiPaolo requested upon taking office on January 4, 1994, was an audit of all funds in the office. The majority of the money that goes through a District Judge's office is cash, and DiPaolo wanted the audit performed as soon as he took over to make sure the books were clean and he would not be blindsided later in the year.

DiPaolo's request was to Pete Freed, the Assistant Court Administrator for the County's District Judges and friend of Carney's. But Freed said the county only audits once a year, and there was no money in the budget to conduct such an audit at that time.

After being turned down by Freed, and believing the request was justified because of the amount of cash that passes through the office, DiPaolo went directly to Erie County Controller Jake Gehrlein and President Judge Jiuliante. Besides, DiPaolo knew Carney for many years and wanted to make sure he was not stepping into a bees nest his first year in office.

The audit was conducted in January and four months later, in May, it was determined that Carney stole over one thousand dollars in marriage license fees from the office. The audit was from Carney taking office in April 1993 through December 1993, when he left.

"His explanation was that he thought he was allowed to keep the money as nobody taught him otherwise at school before he took office," DiPaolo said. "Yeah, right. District Judges are salaried employees of the state. We are not entitled to 'tips.' We are not waiters!"

In a newspaper article, the reporter had asked Peter Freed if Carney would be charged. "His buddy Freed responded that if there was an impropriety, that's up to the D.A.," DiPaolo said. "So, as far as Freed was concerned, it showed he stole the money but that isn't an impropriety?"

Carney, who said he had officiated at 73 marriages in eight months, added that he was the only District Judge who would perform ceremonies in homes, halls, parks, beaches, the zoo and even at 3 a.m. at the Erie County Prison.

"Wow! What a guy?' DiPaolo said. "He should have opened a little chapel like in Vegas. Who in their right fucking mind would go to the county jail at 3 a.m. to marry convicts?"

In June 1994, Carney was charged with 29 counts of failure to make lawful disposition of funds received. In other words, he kept the money from the marriages, putting it in his pocket. He was facing a maximum penalty of 29 years in jail, and fines totally $72,500. As the law required, he would appear before the District Judge where the crime occurred. That would have been DiPaolo, who wisely recused himself.

Attorney Ian Murray, who represented Carney, claimed Carney was innocent and wanted to repay the money to the county. But District Attorney Rusty Cunningham said although that was fine, he would still prosecute and offer a plea deal.

"As always, that was a smoke screen from Cunningham," DiPaolo said. Carney paid $2,151 in fines and cost and the cost of the audit. "They used the excuse that some years prior to that, District Judges, then called aldermen, were permitted to keep any money given to them for weddings and that Carney apparently was merely mixed up and thought the practice was still allowed."

"What bullshit. When there were aldermen, they were not on salary They got paid for what they did, including weddings. And that was 30 years ago, when Carney would have been a kid."

According to DiPaolo, Ian Murray, known as Mr. Super-delegate, was going around town, beating his chest and saying how he got his buddy Carney off.

"But, karma is a bitch," DiPaolo said. "Four months later, while in the Public Defender's Office, Murray was charged with indecent assault of a 21 year old girl. He got a kiss on that one like Carney. But his reputation was never the same."

Robbie Fabrizi, Larry's son would run for Erie School Board, and was a School Director for over twenty years. Even though DiPaolo and Robbie ran against each other in 1993, they still remain friends. DiPaolo always had alot of respect for Judge Larry Fabrizi.

CHAPTER **11**

WORKING WITH THE MEDIA: "A GOOD RELATIONSHIP"

For many years, DiPaolo's relationship with the news media was a symbiotic one.

As a cop, as a homicide investigator, DiPaolo understood that the media had an important role to play in criminal probes, and that the media could indeed be big help to the cops if handled correctly. At least, it was DiPaolo's belief that he could keep reporters from being a hindrance! DiPaolo's aim was to develop and nurture relationships of mutual trust and cooperation with certain reporters, with each side benefiting from the said relationship.

For the most part, it worked. And worked well.

"Young police reporters were always bugging me on homicide cases that I was investigating," the former cop DiPaolo recalls. "I usually told them that I could give out information on certain cases that were ongoing, but absolutely nothing that would jeopardize the cases."

Yes, DiPaolo wanted to use the media as much as possible to further the cause of criminal justice, but for obvious reasons, he did not want certain information attributed to him. In an atmosphere of professional jealousy that often existed at police headquarters, DiPaolo was savvy enough to know it was never wise to let anyone know he was friendly with the media or talking with reporters.

In fact, DiPaolo set those ground rules with young reporters from the start, warning them that if they ever violated DiPaolo's confidence or trust in them, their relationship would end and DiPaolo would never discuss a case or speak with them again.

DiPaolo had earlier cultivated trusting relationships with a number of local reporters, including Jeff Pinski of the Morning News, and Paul Corbran, Tony Pasquale, and Vicki Fabrizio of the Erie Daily Times. They usually had first crack at DiPaolo. In the interest of fair play, DiPaolo would toss each a bone and give whatever information he could. As for the TV reporters, DiPaolo always chose Carol Pella of WSEE, Lou Baxter of WJET and Hyle Richmond and Paul Wagner of WICU.

But things changed!

And even when DiPaolo left the Erie Bureau of Police to become an elected District Judge, his relationship and rapport with the media and especially certain reporters was excellent. When those news reporters called, DiPaolo was willing to share whatever information he could. He knew the law as it applied in such matters, and also believed in the public's right to know. DiPaolo trusted the media in general and in particular those reporters which he dealt with, especially Tim Hahn of the Erie paper later in the Judge's career.

In 2002, however, that trust was challenged and put to the supreme test. This also taught DiPaolo a valuable lesson about human nature and that the slimier side of humanity wasn't always found in just the bad guys he dealt with on the daily basis.

There were plenty of others on the far societal peripheral that a dedicated cop needed to be wary about. One turned out to be Ed Palattella, a relatively new reporter with the Erie Daily Times.

It all began when Italo Cappabianca, a longtime popular Democratic Party Pennsylvania State Representative, died while still in office. It meant Cappabianca's State Assembly seat was not only open and must be filled for the remainder of his term, but would then also be up for grabs in the upcoming elections. DiPaolo was often mentioned for the job, but he was happy where he was, serving in the capacity of a District Judge.

A number of local West Erie Democrats coveted that seat, but it was Gayle Wright, a former Erie City Councilwoman, who strangely opposed

Cappabianca's wife, Linda, and won the appointment to serve for the remainder of Cappabianca's two-year term.

Why strange? Because in Erie, Pennsylvania, for some unexplained reason, it has long been tradition for the widow of an elected male office holder to be appointed to serve out the remainder of her husband's term, if she so desired. It was seen by many almost as a holy right of the mourning widow. (Later, when the popular Erie County Councilman Phil Fatica unexpectedly passed away, Councilman Fiore Leone led the charge to appoint his wife, Kathy, to the vacant council seat, which she might have forgotten as she campaigned against Leone later while both were in office.)

As a result, this unholy opposition by Gayle Wright to Linda Cappabianca simply inheriting her husband's seat created the sourest of notes in the orchestra of Erie's loud and boisterous Democratic Party politics.

Many of the deceased Italo Cappabianca's former supporters were understandably more than just merely upset with Wright's apparently denial of the seat to Mrs. Cappabianca. As their thinking went – the widow had first dibbs! And now, Gayle Wright had denied Linda her first dibbs!

Ironically, if Wright would have waited until the next cycle's election, odds are she might have won the seat on her own and for as long as she wanted to hold onto it.

Being a Democratic Party incumbent in the City of Erie is pretty much a position for life.

But now, as a result of Mrs. Wright's usurping of Linda's 'right' to hold office, there was such discontent among West Erie Democrats, many of them Italian and with allegiances to the Cappabiancas.

And, since Linda Cappabianca had decided not to run for a full term, these Cappabianca faithful found themselves looking past Wright, who had cut in line in front of the widow and for a viable candidate to run against her in next primary election.

They found a winner. Florindo "Flo" Fabrizio, a handsome, deep-voiced former stock-broker who had served as Erie County Clerk for 20 years, was the perfect candidate for these Italian westsiders. Fabrizio was born and educated in Erie. A graduate of Penn State University, he began his career as a public school teacher before getting his broker's license and then transitioning to Democratic Party politics.

What a fit for the Cappabianca Dems to run against Wright!

But unfortunately for DiPaolo, this left him in an untenable position right in the middle of the campaign. Attorney Donald Wright, Gayle's husband, had been one of DiPaolo's closest friends. Furthermore, DiPaolo had grown up with Fabrizio and over the years they, too, had become fast pals and golfed together.

When DiPaolo first ran for elective office – the Sixth Ward District Judge's seat – in 1993, both Don Wright and Flo Fabrizio had served on his campaign's executive committee.

What to do, DiPaolo lamented to himself!

"What a pickle I found myself in!" DiPaolo confided. "So I just told both of them I was staying out of this race. It was just not worth losing the friendship of either of these men who I had come of age with."

Every Friday night, a group of people went out to dinner prior to 2002 and the Wright's and Fabrizio's were in the group as the DiPaolo's invited them. Needless to say, the group got smaller after the election.

DiPaolo's maturity in the matter, and his sense of neutrality seemed to be working! Well, almost. The previous long-term friendship between the DiPaolos and the Wrights was strained ever since.

But in April of 2002, about a month before the primary election, DiPaolo was the recipient of a troubling telephone call from another longtime friend and political ally.

It was from Erie County Councilman Fiore Leone, who had also served on DiPaolo's past executive committee and who was now running Flo Fabrizio's election campaign.

Leone advised DiPaolo that it would be in his best interest to immediately contact Luigi Pasquale, then the Erie County purchasing agent.

"You need to hear firsthand what he just told me," Leone confided to DiPaolo. "Give him a call!"

Once on the phone with DiPaolo, it didn't take long for Pasquale to get right to the point and the reason Councilman Leone was so concerned.

"That Times reporter, Ed Palattella, he came into my office and showed me an envelope," Pasquale began. The envelope contained the return address, "Committee to Elect Flo Fabrizio," but the addressee had been redacted.

The postmark was Erie, Pa., along with a 32-cent postage meter stamp, the kind that businesses and individuals use when they have much U.S. postage business to conduct or mass mailings to send out.

Palattella wanted Pasquale to check the meter number to determine whether the machine used for this mailing was from District Judge DiPaolo's official judicial office.

"I can tell from just looking at the number that that metered stamp machine isn't even assigned to Erie County machines," Pasquale told Palattella and related the conversation to DiPaolo over the phone.

But Palattella nonetheless still demanded that the county purchasing agent check the 12-digit meter number which is printed on every envelope that passes through metered machines, Pasquale told DiPaolo.

"He said he was 100 percent sure that you were letting Fabrizio use your official county postage meter machine to mail Fabrizio's campaign materials and letters asking for political contributions," Pasquale told DiPaolo.

Such a practice, of course, would have a been a most severe breach of ethics and violation of DiPaolo's oath of office, not to mention numerous Pennsylvania campaign laws. No one could be that dumb to use their own assigned postage meter for personal reasons, let alone a world-savvy former top police detective. (The sole occasion in 24 years on the bench when a personal letter was inadvertently mixed with the office business mail by a secretary, DiPaolo immediately notified the county executive and president judge.) Pasquale told DiPaolo he disappeared into the recesses of his office, waited several minutes, then returned to Palattella and told him, "Absolutely not! It's not even the same metered company!"

But Palattella still wanted the serial number from DiPaolo's machine.

"I told him to go to your office to get it from you."

DiPaolo shook his head, ended the phone connection, and waited. How he would handle Palattella's request in person, he had not yet decided. But he would deal with it when it happened. And so he waited. And waited. A day went by. Two. Three. A week. Then several weeks. Then months.

Naturally with the detective instinct DiPaolo had, he asked Pasquale if he would check out his stamp meter totals for the last six months to see if the average of use was about the same, in case Palattella wrote some kind of crazy story.

Days later, Pasquale called DiPaolo and informed him they were all about the same amount, and in fact in April amount Palattella was checking on was down from the rest of the months, not a lot of use.

But, as DiPaolo expected following the conversation with Pasquale, Palattella never showed up at the District Judge's office. DiPaolo then decided to remain quiet about this information, and not to confront the reporter with what he knew. Not then. Not yet.

Several months after the May primary, in which Flo Fabrizio won the nomination by defeating Wright, and eventually would win the general election, DiPaolo was handling judicial action against defendants accused in the recent armed robbery of a Pennsylvania State Store. In Pennsylvania at the time, wine and hard alcohol could be purchased only from state-owned and operated liquor stores, a throwback to Prohibition of the 1920s and early 1930s. Since then, wine and beer are now available in grocery stores and some convenience stores.

It was summer and the newspaper reporter was telephoning DiPaolo's judicial office and requesting information about the robbery case. As soon as DiPaolo picked up the phone, he recognized Palattella's voice, distinctive to the judge through an apparent and distinctive speech impediment.

"This is Ed Palattella, Judge," the caller immediately said, his tone friendly and respectful. "I need some information on that armed robbery you're handling." He was apparently assigned to the story and had no choice but to call DiPaolo for the information. It must have been an unhappy moment.

"Wait a minute," DiPaolo said. "Now you want to be nice to me because you want me to help you out with your story? Silence.

"But just a few months ago you tried to throw me under the bus, falsely claiming to others that you had information that I was allowing Flo Fabrizio to use my official postage meter machine for his campaign? And now you need me? Is that what you're saying?"

DiPaolo said Palattella began to stammer. "I had to follow up on the information I was given," DiPaolo quoted the reporter, while seeing it as his feeble offering at an attempt to explain his actions. DiPaolo instantly knew who gave the reporter the made-up story. An Erie School District Administrator who also claimed Leone and Fabrizio were losers. Obviously, the snitch could never be a political analyst!

"That's fine," DiPaolo said. "But why didn't you come straight to me at my office and ask to see my machine for yourself? That way, if it matched your envelope, well, then you would have had me!

"But no, you went behind my back and tried to stick it in my ass when we were supposed to have a mutual trust. Don't you ever call me again, either here at my office or at my home. You are nothing but a fucking hair lip rat!" And with those last words, Judge DiPaolo hung up. Afterward, DiPaolo regretted mentioning Palattella's speech impediment, but he had been very upset. It was the first of many clashes between the two that would last for many years.

CHAPTER 12

MAY 2, 2007
THE G-MEN COMMETH

Cold sweats.

The federal prosecutor in charge had a gut-wrenching case of the jitters. It was not unusual for him. He always got that way, nervous perspiration, even on the coldest of days, and elevated heart rate, as it were, just before leading his crew of G-Men into action, into those dangerous crime-busting situations of folk lore and dramatic Silver Screen and TV fantasies.

He thought, "what the hell, that's what they are paid to do",.... risk body and limb for God and Country. They were indeed paid very well as far as law enforcement wages go, much better than most police agencies. His crew was college-educated, highly-trained, the best of the best. Like many of his ilk, he harbored a professional job snobbery common to those at the perceived top level of law-enforcement's pecking order. And why shouldn't he? After all, his job, regardless of the risk, was to shield from the really bad guys the citizenry of America, and especially those poor souls in that hotbed of spies, discontents, insurgents and political sedition – Erie, Pennsylvania?

That's why, he kept reassuring himself, he and his federal agents got the really big bucks.

On this typically balmy May evening in Erie in 2007, the fearless, albeit sweaty crew of crack agents from the vaunted U.S. Federal Bureau of Investigation was poised to strike again. To a man, from federal prosecutor to the greenest probie, they knew their planned raid could possibly be the last they would make into the jaws unspeakable terror.

Ah, but the heights of glory, especially the self-infatuated type, hath no limits.

Earlier that evening, the feds risked detection to scope out their evening target.

They passed almost unnoticed as they drove and walked the streets of Southwest Erie through the quiet, modest, but well-kept middle-class residential neighborhood in Erie's sprawling Sixth Ward.

Residents planting their spring annuals in hopes of an early summer, or mowing their lawns for the first time after one of Erie's legendary and typical long and snowy winters, unsuspectingly waved to the well-dressed federal sleuths who walked or drove by. Some of the neighbors, who were still raking matted fall leaves as part of their annual spring cleanup ritual, paused briefly to observe vehicles not familiar to the neighborhood as they slowly drove past and down one street and up another. This was a friendly neighborhood, those occupying the neat homes returned quickly to their annual chores, totally unaware of the danger lurking in their midst.

Laughter of children at play resonated throughout the area as the Feds went about their surreptitious business at hand. They smiled awkwardly, without sincerity, at the children, all of whom were unknowing of what would come later. With daylight hours growing longer with each passing spring day, kids now played outside before and after their dinners, taking advantage of the newfound tepid temperatures, while the older residents tended to their lawn chores and enjoyed the soft spring Lake Erie breezes wafting southward from the recently frozen, and now-thawed body of water just to their north.

But the feds were unmoved by the weather. Or the friendliness of the neighborhood. Vigilant to their mission to a fault, they were.

Stopping their black undercover vehicles periodically to snap photographs of the target residence, and especially of what they suspected to be stealth-like comings and goings there, they were as thorough as their founder, the deceased J. Edgar Hoover, would expect them to be.

All was carefully planned and orchestrated with by-the-book precision by these extraordinary professionals who would again risk life and limb this very evening to protect the American Way and all the residents of Southwest Erie, Pennsylvania. Yes, the lead agent thought with smug satisfaction, this would be an operation for the books! With a smile, he thought of the headlines in the morning paper. And he thought of his boss in Pittsburgh. She would be so satisfied!

Still, he grew even more nervous than usual. Almost fearful. Who could blame him for his fretting on this fateful night, and for being so unnerved? No one, he thought, again with that sense of self-appreciation. He gulped in a few deep breaths of Erie's springtime oxygen and slowly exhaled with a whoosh and an exclaimed "Whew!"

Just get the job done, he thought. Soon, it all would be over. It would go well. It had to! After all, he was leading a legendary F.B.I. assault! And soon, the glory would be this and that of his team – another win for the good guys; another victory on the side of law and order and justice in the perpetual battle against horrific evil.

But the clock was ticketing. And zero hour was almost here!

CHAPTER 13

———————■———————

MAY 2, 2007
THE PITTSBURGH ERIE CONNECTION
TWO HOURS TO GO

Slightly more than 100 miles due south of Erie via Interstate-79 or U.S. Route 19 sits the federal building in Pittsburgh, Pennsylvania.

Late that Wednesday afternoon, the U.S. Attorney for the Western District of Pennsylvania sat alone in her office, pondering the pending F.B.I. action she had authorized to take place that evening in Erie, a city that fell under her jurisdiction.

Appointed six years earlier by President George W. Bush, this registered Republican was the first woman and youngest person ever to hold the top federal prosecutorial post in the Keystone State.

She was considered by many to be the most controversial U.S. Attorneys in the history of Pennsylvania, as she split her time between running the Pittsburgh office and as acting director of the Justice Department's Office on Violence Against Women in Washington, D.C. To her, Erie was merely an outpost of the Pittsburgh office. Yet nothing the Feds did in Erie took place without her knowledge and prior approval. Nothing.

Although some would say politics never play a role in alleged criminal investigations conducted by the federal government, others would insist just the opposite. And on this spring evening in the city by the lake, a whopper of a political farce and injustice was about to take place in a quiet residential neighborhood.

The U.S. Attorney of the Western District of Pennsylvania was aware of all that would be at stake that evening. Of the lives that would be impacted. Only she did not care who got hurt. Especially if the target was a leading figure in the local Democratic Party.

While the U.S. Attorney for the Western District of Pennsylvania mulled the coming F.B.I. action more than 100 miles away, a county prosecutor in Erie was having the same thoughts.

The Republican Erie County District Attorney not only knew what was about to take place in that quiet neighborhood, but also helped to arrange the evening's activities.

Brad Foulk knew exactly what was coming down. He relished the thought of what was about to take place, and could not wait to spill what he knew to his favorite newspaper reporter.

Foulk knew that being in the same political party as the leading federal prosecutor was a huge plus for him. Together with the his federal counterpart in Pittsburgh, they could make life difficult for members of the opposite party – even those in the judiciary. He smiled at the thought, as the clock ticked toward the F.B.I. raid.

Despite it being broad daylight with neighbors everywhere, neighbors with rakes, neighbors with pruning shearers, neighbors with bedding geraniums, neighbors with lawn-mowers, despite all the activity, the black vehicle came to conspicuous stop directly in the middle of the southwest Erie street.

Neighbors paused to stare as the well-dressed many in a conservative business suit held a camera out the passenger-side window and began photographing the home and those who were either entering or emerging from it.

And then, just as quickly as it had stopped in the middle of the street, blocking all traffic in both directors, the black sedan bolted forward and disappeared around the first corner.

Michael Romeo was tired. It had been a long day teaching school, and he was anxious to get home to spend time with his family before his wife departed for an evening engagement with her friends and other family members.

Romeo picked up his kids at his in-laws' home. They would all have family dinner together. But as he pulled away from the house, he got the sense something was different. Something was amiss.

Now, Romeo was not a cop, and he had no police training. But he had keen instincts, especially when his children were with him. Almost immediately, he sensed he was being followed. In his rear-view mirror, and he picked up the "tail," a small, black sedan. Each time Michael turned the corner, the sedan attempted to follow. Yet through a series of rapid maneuvers and twists and turns, it was not long before his "tail" was left in the dust.

Only later would Romeo recall being followed that evening, and by whom.

And he would be resentful that during an innocent ride home, his young children were made to be pawns in an elaborate federal scheme, one with its roots deeply immersed in politics. His son, Gino, was only six at the time; his daughter, Gianna, just three and riding in car seats.

"Simply amazing!" DiPaolo would later say. "These Feds are such nitwits."

CHAPTER 14

---■---

MAY 2, 2007
PETTY POLITICAL JEALOUSY
UGLY POLITICAL "HIT"

In hindsight, DiPaolo later believed it was inevitable that petty political jealousy would rear its ugly head against him. But even DiPaolo was surprised that it would come from the supposed good guys.

He had always sensed that eventually his life-long unblemished tough-guy, law-and-order image take a hit from the criminals he routinely put away under lock and key. Not much could sneak up on DiPaolo at this point in his public life, but taking a personal political hit from those assigned to protect society from criminal behavior was unexpected, although not totally surprising.

DiPaolo had long been aware of the foul stench of unsavory politics, not only locally on occasion, but from some federal quarters in law enforcement as well. But that warm spring evening in 2007 would forever not only harden that speculation, but confirm in his mind the feds as the worst of the worst for all time to come.

That Wednesday evening, DiPaolo was at his office at 5:15 p.m., preparing paperwork for an upcoming meeting of his Juvenile Diversion Program. It was not unusual for him to be at work by 6 a.m., and still be at his desk more than 12 hours later.

The phone rang. In those days before Caller-ID, DiPaolo knew it was either the police calling for legal advice, or to schedule an arraignment or hearing. It had been another long day, and he was anxious to finish his work, but he also knew the call could be important. It was. And it was devastating, not just to DiPaolo, but more importantly, to his family.

It was Janet. And his wife was in tears.

Janet, a deeply religious mother and grandmother whose smile and youthful appearance belied more than half her 60 years married to a cop and judge. She was not only in tears, but also anger. And fear. Mostly fear.

DiPaolo, on the other hand, knew his wife was not easily given over to emotional outbursts. He immediately knew that a serious event had transpired. He bristled; an automatic reaction that occurred whenever he sensed a member of his family had been hurt or wronged.

This sixth sense never betrayed him.

Janet had been hosting a "Spring Party" in the DiPaolo's West Erie home. In attendance were longtime friends and family members. It was one of those "gals only" events routinely held by thousands of women across the city, the state and the country. Gathered in the DiPaolo home was a cross-sampling of women reflective of the Erie community: The mother of an out-of-state F.B.I. Agent; public and private school administrators; the spouse of a popular Pennsylvania state legislator; high-ranking administrators in law enforcement; professional women; and stay-at-home moms and grandmoms.

Not one of them had their picture posted in a local Post Office. In fact, it would be rare to find even a traffic violation or parking ticket issued to any of the attendees. All were respected in their community, all enjoying the company and friendship of each other and of the evening and the warmth of the DiPaolo home.

What drew them all to this particular home on this particular evening?

The first attraction was genuine genteel camaraderie among friends and family. The second was the discount sale of handbags, jewelry, key chains and sun glasses by a local woman who had conducted many similar sales events in the past.

Such "purse parties," as they are popularly called, have been and remain ongoing throughout the region, state and nation. It is a social staple, not unlike Tupperware, Avon or Cutco.

But, in the midst of this camaraderie and female socializing on a beautiful spring evening, an unexpected and rude interruption:

Suddenly, and without warning – and of course with great fanfare and bullying bluster – a federal raiding posse barged into this mix of "dangerous" Erie women. Led by Assistant United States Attorney Marshall Piccinni, five Federal Bureau of Investigation agents raided DiPaolo's home, alleging "knock-off" counterfeit purses were being sold.

By purchasing the purses, the feds claimed, these previously law-abiding mothers and grandmothers were now "aiding terrorism."

Terrorism? Purses? Key chains? That's what they said.

Only later, it was learned the feds in their surveillance of the DiPaolo home had driven around that residential neighborhood, and stopped their suspicious-appearing unmarked vehicles in the middle of the street to take photos of women entering the home as well as record license plate numbers of the party guests' vehicles.

Concerned neighbors began phoning the DiPaolo home and Erie Police Headquarters to report upon these unseemly activities by strangers on their quiet block.

Later, all would learn the suspicious characters turned out to be federal agents. Now, with their clever cover blown, the federal agents hit the well-maintained residence, and Janet quickly phoned her judicial husband.

DiPaolo immediately headed home.

When he got there, he was met by the agent who was then in charge of the operation, a grinning federal terrorist hunter named Kelly M. Smith, who told DiPaolo the agents were not there to upset his wife or her guests.

"Could have fooled me," DiPaolo said.

The agent went on to say they were only after the woman conducting the sale. He said the woman holding the sale had been warned in the past against holding such parties.

DiPaolo was also met by another agent, Scott Brooks.

Although the event was being held in the DiPaolo home's Great Room situated in the basement, Janet DiPaolo and the party organizer, Sharon Lytle, were at the kitchen table. Agent Smith asked them, "Where are the Marinos?" When Janet answered that there were no Marinos present, Lytle identified herself and said, "I'm conducting this party."

"You know these purses are counterfeit and you are aiding terrorism!" Smith told the women.

But Lytle explained many were simply "seconds."

Still grinning, Smith said, "We will see. But we still have to confiscate them."

It was crystal clear he was more than enjoying himself and the moment, even relishing in it. Law and order was triumphing. Oh, the glory.

The DiPaolos' daughter, Dawn DiPaolo-Romeo, who appeared from the basement gathering, asked, "Instead of you going down there and freaking everyone out, can I simply bring the purses up to you?"

"Fine," Smith smiled with a smug and condescending attitude that said "I can be accommodating when I have to be."

"What will you do with these purses?" Janet DiPaolo asked. "Will Sharon get them back?"

Pointing a finger toward the ceiling, Smith smiled broadly. "We send them to the big shredder in the sky!" And then, unable to contain himself at his clever humor, he laughed.

Daughter Dawn, along with the DiPaolo's daughter-in-law, Beth, enlisted the help of several friends to retrieve nine large cargo bags, each filled with purses, which the feds collected and took outside. Another fed, Amamdi Uche, placed the bags into an unmarked federal SUV at the curb.

"Gee, Judge, you have a beautiful home and it's so well-landscaped," Agent Uche said, as though the weakly inspired compliment would make the evening a success and all would feel better about it.

But it remained not far from DiPaolo's mindset that this raid, and the later news media coverage, was not pulled off with the purpose of eliminating the counterfeiting of goods, or stamping out the practice of local women assisting terrorists. Rather, DiPaolo knew the sole purpose of this clumsily-executed event was entirely political in nature, staged solely to embarrass the Magisterial Judge as political payback.

DiPaolo knew from past experiences with the feds that no Assistant U.S. Attorney could make any kind of a move without first getting the approval of the U.S. Attorney with jurisdiction over the region. In these local cases in Western Pennsylvania, the assistants answer to U.S. Attorney Mary Beth Buchanan, a Republican.

From her office in Pittsburgh, Pennsylvania, Buchanan okayed what DiPaolo now knew was a gross miscarriage of justice directed solely at him, but at the expense of his wife, daughter, daughter-in-law, and their friends. It had been common knowledge in law enforcement circles, locally and even nationally, that Buchanan was fond of targeting Democratic office-holders.

CHAPTER 15

MAY 2, 2007
D-DAY PLUS ONE HOUR

Smith and Brooks now had Lytle on the DiPaolo's patio, where they sat at the table and interrogated the party organizer.

DiPaolo, from his days as a cop and having observed the F.B.I.'s method of operation in the past, knew the feds never tape-recorded their interrogations. DiPaolo believed they didn't want such firm evidence to keep them from putting misleading information in their 302 Investigative Reports, especially accurate information relevant to what the subject actually said or did not say.

This now was no different.

As the feds gathered up their haul of purses and began to leave, followed by Lytle, DiPaolo wondered just what kind of a raid had taken place. He knew that when "real" cops were engaged in raids, they confiscated not only the alleged illegal items, but also any money being used to purchase the goods. For example, if cops found a kilo of cocaine in a drug raid, does anyone think they would leave behind the $50,000 in cash also found at the scene? Also, in this instance, since the feds believed the purses were counterfeit, why weren't the other items for sale at the home checked out as well? It did not make much sense to the former veteran cop. But in his mind, the smell of a ruse was starting to take form … and reek.

DiPaolo knew that during his career as a Detective Sergeant, during which he conducted hundreds of raids on homes, there was never such a shoddy one as these Feds had undertaken.

CHAPTER **16**

MAY 3, 2007
THE THICKENING PLOT

At eight the next morning, Thursday, May 3, 2007, Attorney Tony Logue, Chief Public Defender of Erie County, telephoned the judge. Logue, a longtime good friend of DiPaolo and his family, asked, "What the hell went on at your house last night?"

"Why?" the judge asked. "Was something on the news?"

"Not yet," Logue said, adding that while having coffee that morning at a shop between the Erie County and U.S. District Courthouses, he ran into a newspaper reporter. The Erie Times-News reporter, Ed Palattella, whom DiPaolo knew to be close with both Assistant U.S. Attorney Piccinni and Erie County District Attorney Brad Foulk, told Logue that DiPaolo's house was raided by the F.B.I. for counterfeit purses, according to Logue.

According to Attorney Logue, his coffee shop encounter with Palattella was around 7:30 a.m., which DiPaolo knew was a full 60 minutes before the two courthouses opened at 8:30 that morning. It did little to alter DiPaolo's feeling that the raid was a ruse to embarrass him. The reporter also knew and told Logue that no one was going to be charged, but that Palattella was still going to write a story about what happened anyway. DiPaolo now wondered how the reporter could know that no charges would be filed.

Later that morning, Janet DiPaolo telephoned her husband and reported that while cleaning the Great Room, she discovered a number of additional bags of purses that Lytle had not displayed prior to the arrival of the federal agents the previous evening.

When DiPaolo arrived home around lunch time, he saw there were seven large zipped up cargo bags, each filled with purses. He also saw in open view of anyone in the room other merchandise such as jewelry, sunglasses and key chains, as well as an envelope with cash and checks.

The judge immediately telephoned Piccinni at the U.S. Attorney's Office and advised the federal official of the purses and other merchandise the agents had left behind. He asked Piccinni to have one of the agents retrieve all the items at once. But Piccinni told DiPaolo he was only interested in the purses.

DiPaolo previously knew Piccinni from the federal lawyer's days as an assistant Erie County District Attorney. In fact, Piccinni had been assigned to DiPaolo's Magisterial District Courtroom as the ADA for Central Court.

Because of the prior professional relationship, DiPaolo felt it appropriate to ask the question that had been haunting him all night:

"Was this necessary?" DiPaolo asked.

Piccinni was quick to reply, leading DiPaolo to think the answer had been rehearsed. The fed attorney said his agents had searched for Lytle in her van for two days prior to the raid. The first lie?

"We wanted to grab her before she got to your house, Judge. But we couldn't find her."

"And you were a part of this?" DiPaolo asked.

DiPaolo recalls the federal attorney at first hesitating, but then saying, "Well they (F.B.I.) came to me and I happened to be in the neighborhood as I dropped my kid off at school soccer practice. So, I just drove by." Yet, DiPaolo knew this fed lived in Edinboro, Pennsylvania, some 15 miles south of the DiPaolo home. Strange that the school practice would be that far away? Lie No. 2?

Piccinni actually could not deny being there since he was seen driving by. The judge's daughter, Dawn, who had worked for her father for years and knew Piccinni from his court appearances, was standing in front of the judge's house, waiting for her husband to pick up and take their children to dinner when she observed Piccinni drive by. At the time, she never gave it a second thought. It was common in the neighborhood to observe those you were familiar with, but who might not live nearby. But DiPaolo could now only roll his eyes, thinking of a federal super sleuth in action.

After hearing Piccinni's eyebrow-raising account of the previous evening, DiPaolo waited for the feds to pick up the left-behind purses. Agent Amamdi Uche got there at 12:45 p.m.

DiPaolo himself carried the bags up the basement stairs and out onto the rear patio, then helped Uche carry the seven bags to his unmarked SUV. It took three trips, during which Uche again advised DiPaolo he was sorry the event took place, and again said, "You have such a beautiful home."

But when DiPaolo attempted to hand over to the agent a large box filled with sunglasses, jewelry, cash and checks, Uche said, "Well, Marshall only wants me to pick up the purses."

Over the course of the next several days, DiPaolo began to piece together the puzzle. It did not take much detective work to uncover the loosely-disguised and ill-prepared federal plan apparently designed not to catch terrorists, but solely to embarrass the former city cop, and now Judge.

Later, DiPaolo learned from his son-in-law, Michael Romeo, that after picking up his children and while driving to McGarrey's Oakwood Café for dinner, Romeo sensed he was being followed by a man in a small car. Romeo, who at that time had no idea of the pending raid, described the man in the car as being white and wearing glasses. (Later, DiPaolo determined it was Agent Brooks.) Romeo had little trouble, he later said, making a few quick turns and shaking the federal tail before taking his kids to dinner.

By now, DiPaolo could only marvel at the F.B.I.'s keen and stealthy investigative skills, being "made" while following a dad and his two small children on their way to dinner – and then actually being shaken! Even more, DiPaolo wondered what these agents thought of his son-in-law and grandchildren – more terrorists with purses?

CHAPTER 17

MAY 4-5, 2007
SURPRISE! THE NEWSPAPER
HAS THE STORY!

The next day, Friday, May 4, as was expected, Reporter Palattella contacted Judge DiPaolo for a statement. DiPaolo could have responded with "no comment" and let it go at that. But he believed that the reporter would simply spin it the way he wanted. DiPaolo had past experience with this reporter and had reason to seriously question his accuracy. But DiPaolo felt morally obligated to make a statement – and hope he wouldn't get hurt that much by it.

Also, as expected, the banner headline on the front page in the Erie paper the following morning screamed about the F.B.I. crashing a purse party in the home of Judge DiPaolo. DiPaolo knew it had been a mistake talking to the reporter, but he did not regret doing what he believed was the right thing.

The one hurt the most by the story, of course, was DiPaolo's wife, Janet. She was upset and embarrassed, and felt that for the first time his 40 years of public life he was getting slaughtered because she had agreed to host a purse party.

But DiPaolo again took the high road. "Look, don't worry about it," he smiled. "We'll get through this."

DiPaolo assured Janet they were not going to hide in embarrassment. They had done nothing wrong, and had nothing to be ashamed of. Although they got blasted in the news media, including the local television stations, which picked up the story from the newspaper, it was not the first purse party and probably will not be the last held in the privacy of an individual's home. They were being held all over Erie County; in fact, all over the United States!

Later that day, at the 5 p.m. Mass at Sacred Heart Church, where the DiPaolos had long been important pillars of that Roman Catholic community, they were approached by many concerned parishioners. All were supportive.

"Are those Feds nuts?" one woman, eye-brows raised, asked.

When Mass ended, another woman approached DiPaolo. "I hope Jerry Clark wasn't one of those F.B.I. Agents at your house," the woman began.

DiPaolo, who knew F.B.I. Agent Clark from Clark's days as a County Probation Officer, said, "No Ma'am. He wasn't one of the feds present."

"Good to hear!" the woman said. "But why do you ask?" DiPaolo wanted to know. Do you know him?

"I sure do because just a few months ago I was at his house with his mother and his aunt. His wife, Danielle, was hosting one of those same purse parties that night. Heck, I even bought two of them!"

"Excuse me?" said DiPaolo, not sure he heard her words correctly. "Are you saying that F.B.I. Agent Gerry Clark's wife hosted a purse party at their house?" DiPaolo was incredulous.

"Yes, sir! I was there!" "Who else was there," DiPaolo managed to stammer. "There were other women there who were the wives of other F.B.I. Agents, and also Danielle's friends."

It took DiPaolo a long moment to process this startling information. DiPaolo looked at Janet in amazement.

He thought for a moment: Clark was actually the only agent from the Erie office of the Federal Bureau of Investigation who wasn't present at DiPaolo's home the night of the daring purse raid. DiPaolo was slowly beginning to confirm many of his earlier thoughts. He had been set up.

CHAPTER **18**

MAY 7-12, 2007
PALATTELLA SPREADING MORE
MISINFORMATION & UNTRUTHS

The following Monday, May 7, 2007, DiPaolo's good friend Tony Logue, the lawyer, again telephoned to tell DiPaolo he encountered the newspaper reporter Palattella that morning at the Erie County Courthouse where Logue served as the county's Chief Public Defender.

Logue said he was told by Palattella that Janet DiPaolo was out delivering purses over the weekend to women who had bought them but left the purses behind at the DiPaolo house after the Feds' raid.

"That's bullshit, Tony! Totally untrue!" DiPaolo hotly responded. Wherever he got that he is full of shit.

The next day, Tuesday, May 8, Vicki Fabrizio, wife of Pennsylvania State Representative Flo Fabrizio, visited the DiPaolo home to ask Janet whether Vicki's new recently-purchased purse was still there. Janet told Vicki she was the only guest who'd left a purchased purse behind, and gave her the purse.

"I was wondering what you were going to do – deliver them or what?" Fabrizio continued. "I figured you had a lot. I was telling Brad (District Attorney Brad Foulk) how scared we were."

Later, after Janet relayed this conversation to her husband at home, DiPaolo telephoned Vicki Fabrizio

After exchanging small-talk pleasantries, DiPaolo quickly got to the point. "Vicki, tell me about the conversation you had with Brad last Friday night."

She told DiPaolo that she and her husband had gone to the local Democratic Party's annual Jefferson-Jackson Dinner that night and the District Attorney had joined them at their table.

"He asked whether the women were upset at Janet DiPaolo's house Wednesday night. I told him, 'Wow, that was something! Women were running all over not knowing what to do.' He said, 'Poor Janet – I didn't know until about 1 o'clock that afternoon what was going on.'"

Fabrizio said she told Foulk she had purchased a purse at the party, but left it there and did not know whether Janet was going to deliver the purses over the weekend or how she would get the purses to the women who purchased them.

"First off," DiPaolo asked Vicki, "how did Foulk know you were there? You never mentioned it. He was the one who asked you about being there."

DiPaolo guessed that Fabrizio's inaccurate assumption to Foulk about Janet delivering purses was passed on from Foulk to the newspaper reporter, who then relayed the same incorrect information to Attorney Logue that Monday morning. DiPaolo felt his beliefs were now confirmed; and that this was typical of the reporter in question: passing along incorrect and unsubstantiated information.

"Oh my God! I'm so sorry," Fabrizio told DiPaolo. "I did not realize any of this."

"Look," DiPaolo told both the Fabrizios, "Foulk is a piece of shit. It's my belief he is behind the entire incident. His 'Poor Janet' remark was just an act. Fuck him and his buddy Piccinni!"

Unfortunately, friendship became another victim of the purse raid. The previous close relationship between the DiPaolos and the Fabrizios was never the same after that day.

The following Wednesday, May 9, Attorney Tim Lucas, a former Prosecutor and then highly sought-after criminal defense lawyer, phoned DiPaolo to say he might be representing Lytle if needed.

After meeting with the purse lady, Lucas told DiPaolo he phoned federal attorney Piccinni to inquire about any legal action that might be taken on the part of the Feds against his client.

"Piccinni told me he assigned the case to Assistant U.S. Attorney Christine Sanner. He suggested to me that I talk with her," Lucas related to DiPaolo. DiPaolo now believed Piccinni had dropped his involvement in this steadily growing, unseemly event; that he did what he had to do for DA Foulk.

When Lucas contacted Sanner, he told her that Lytle was willing to cooperate. He told Sanner that if the Feds wanted names of others who had hosted parties, or those from whom Lytle purchased the purses and how often, Lytle would cooperate fully with authorities conducting the investigation. Sanner said she'd get with Marshall and advise him. "Lucas had baited her to determine what her response would be," DiPaolo said.

But later, Sanner called Lucas with a different response to the lawyer's offer to cooperate: "'Ah, that's not necessary,'" Lucas quoted Sanner as saying. "'Just tell her not to have any more parties. Marshall said thanks anyway.'"

When Lucas asked whether charges would be filed against Lytle, the Assistant U.S. Attorney told him, "For now, I don't think so. Just tell her to stop."

So much for counterfeiting. So much for aiding terrorism, DiPaolo thought. But it was Lucas who summoned it up correctly.

"You were set up, Judge," he said. "Lytle had no intention to talk to them. This was just a set-up for the judge. They don't care about her having parties, and that just proved it."

Barely two months had passed since the "raid" when another event put the official stamp of confirmation on all of DiPaolo's suspicions:

It was July 12 when the Chief of Police at Erie International Airport phoned DiPaolo with information that would sting the popular Magisterial Judge. Chief David Bagnoni had been DiPaolo's detective partner for years within the Erie Police Department. The two had been not only detective partners, but also best friends.

It had been Bagnoni, son of the late Erie City Councilman Mario Bagnoni, himself a former cop, who had blown the whistle on a possible gangland plot to kill DiPaolo during a murder investigation a quarter center earlier.

Over the years, although both DiPaolo and Bagnoni had retired from the force and moved on, they remained close friends and confidants.

On this day, Bagnoni told DiPaolo there had been an unfounded report of a bomb in luggage at the airport. Although the report was unfounded, federal aviation law required Bagnoni to notify the F.B.I.. The federal agent who showed up to investigate was the same Scott Brooks.

Bagnoni previously had known Brooks from other investigations, so after their work on the unfounded report was completed, it was not unusual for Bagnoni to invite the Fed to a cup of coffee in the tiny airport restaurant. As small talk filled the air, Bagnoni jokingly commented, "By the way, that was a nice pinch you made of those dangerous 60-year-old grandmothers at that purse party."

Brooks, not knowing of any connection between Bagnoni and DiPaolo, shrugged, "We (F.B.I.) did not want to do that, Chief, but Marshall and Brad insisted that it be done." Brooks shook his head, telling Bagnoni the Feds were "getting heat" from the public, and again insisting the agents did not want any part of conducting the "raid," but that there were others "who had it in for that judge." The message was obvious that Marshall and Brad wanted to embarrass DiPaolo.

DiPaolo had suspected all along that it was Brad Foulk, the Republican District Attorney, who was behind the purse party fiasco. Foulk had it in for DiPaolo for several years and now he had his petty political pay back. Petty, because he shamelessly attacked a lifelong Democrat by embarrassing the office-holder's innocent wife. In fact, DiPaolo knew that after he won his third six-year term in 2005, Foulk bragged that he had to find someone who could beat him the next time. He said he was going to run an Erie ex-cop against DiPaolo, someone who lived just a few blocks away from him.

CHAPTER 19

A FOULK TALE

Brad Foulk, born and raised in Erie and becoming a lawyer in 1975, began consuming alcohol heavily almost immediately upon graduating from high school.

In January 1977, Foulk joined several friends in making the trek to Miami, Florida, to take in that year's Super Bowl. By March, some two months later, he still had not returned home. His frantic mother, Jean Heibel Foulk, asked her own mother, the wealthy Mrs. Grace Heibel, to help locate her darling Bradley. Who did Mrs. Heibel seek out? A young Erie cop who was already making a name for himself as a savvy street investigator who got results.

Dominick DiPaolo was offered the then whopping sum by 1977 standards of $15,000 to travel to Florida and bring back Erie County's future District Attorney. The sum, actually, was more than DiPaolo's annual salary as a City of Erie police officer. But reluctantly, DiPaolo declined the offer. Instead, he put Mrs. Heibel in touch with a national firm, The Blackburn Detective Agency. It did not take long for the private dicks to find Foulk – albeit, drunk on a beach – and return him home to Erie.

It was the start of a pattern of substance rehab after rehab, relapse after relapse, and failure after failure to get and remain sober. Even after his wife left the attorney, he continued to drink.

By the middle1980s, Foulk caught himself a major break when he was appointed as an assistant Erie County Public Defender. By 1986, he remarried and from 1988 to 1995 he worked for his pal, William "Rusty" Cunningham, in the Republican's District Attorney's office.

After Cunningham became an Erie County judge, Foulk parlayed the gig in Cunningham's office to run for DA several years later. Cunningham had been elected District Attorney only after the very popular D.A. Mike Veshecco rolled his car while intoxicated, unfortunately suffering serious injuries that resulted in being paralyzed from the waist down.

As District Attorney, Foulk had the unusual habit of annoying many local cops by taking over their criminal investigations from the start. The cops, however, believed that a District Attorney should not be directing a criminal investigation before suspects have been identified and charges are filed. They believe D.A.s are to take their cases and evidence to court, offering legal advice when needed. Somehow, local attorneys did not seem to mind and allowed Foulk to be both amateur cop and amateur prosecutor. Foulk's sidekick in the office, DiPaolo knew, was Marshall Piccinni, another product of the Cunningham era.

Foulk's supporters in the legal community – defense lawyers who were his buddies – appeared to get special and favorable treatment for their clients from the DA's office. Deals were made in homicide cases, and many felt it was becoming normal operating procedure for some defense attorneys to get their clients' DUI charges reduced to the less serious public intoxication charges.

Early on, the cop and lifelong Democrat DiPaolo got along with the Republican Foulk. But they soon had a major run-in over a criminal investigation that never moved out of the DA's office. DiPaolo later learned that in 1999, Foulk had accepted campaign contributions from the targets of the stalled criminal investigation. When DiPaolo told Foulk he was a dirt-bag and should be ashamed of himself, Foulk merely laughed. After DiPaolo called out Foulk on the contributions, even though Foulk was the incumbent District Attorney and even after DiPaolo had become a District Judge, they never spoke again.

In early 1999, one of Foulk's good friends and his Assistant DA Marshall Piccinni, left Foulk's office to become an appointed Assistant U.S. Attorney. According to Foulk, his longtime Republican pal Tom Ridge, then governor of Pennsylvania, was instrumental in helping Piccinni obtain the federal appointment. Now, between Foulk and Piccinni, they appeared to DiPaolo to feel they ran the entire Erie County Criminal Justice System.

By 2004, however, there was a Democratic governor, Ed Rendell.

DiPaolo's personal and professional friendship with Rendell dated back to Rendell's days as Philadelphia's District Attorney. A homicide investigation in Erie had led DiPaolo to Philly, where the two had immediately connected. Rendell's first assistant at the time had been Bernie Siegel, a former Erie County Assistant Prosecutor who DiPaolo previously worked with on the Louis DiNicola arson/murder case that had initially resulted in the defendant being sentenced to three life terms, plus 20 years. As a result of Rendell's confidence in DiPaolo, the Governor appointed the Sixth Ward District Judge to the prestigious Pennsylvania Commission on Crime and Delinquency. On the commission, DiPaolo was the only District Judge of the 556 in the Commonwealth to have ever been appointed to the august agency. The impressive Commission Membership included Common Pleas Court Judges from Philadelphia, Pittsburgh and Harrisburg, State Senators, Prison Superintendents, Directors of Parole and Probation at the state level, Directors of Domestic Violence and Abused Women Coalitions, County District Attorneys – and, DiPaolo.

In addition, DiPaolo had also been active for decades in many civic, youth, athletic and religious organizations, and was the City of Erie's most decorated police officer ever.

The green-eyed Foulk, however, upon learning of DiPaolo's appointment, was furious. Foulk himself had for several years lobbied for his own appointment to the Commission. Foulk, the chairman of the Erie County "Weed and Seed" program, which derived all of his funding from the Pennsylvania Commission on Crime and Delinquency, confided to several local lawyers that he would try to learn from Rendell why he did not get the coveted appointment – and also attempt to get DiPaolo booted off.

Another Foulk friend was former Erie police officer James Skindell, who had left the department to become head of security at Erie's then new Presque Isle Downs and Casino. The appointment, however, was short-lived. After a background check, the Pennsylvania Gaming Commission rejected his working in that position at the privately owned casino.

DiPaolo later learned that another mutual friend of both Foulk and Skindell, Frank Scozzi, an assistant to an assistant to Erie School District Superintendent, Dr. James Barker, was spreading the word that DiPaolo, who had a disagreement with Skindell years earlier, had written to Governor Rendell seeking to have Skindell fired. DiPaolo also learned that Scozzi claimed to have read a copy of the letter, and Foulk was telling anyone who would listen.

Scozzi had been at a social event at a local stock-broker's home, the home of Greg and Nancy Orlando. In attendance were judges, attorneys and business owners. DiPaolo and his wife, Janet, were also there, but left early to attend another gathering. Early the next day, however, a local judge phoned DiPaolo to ask if DiPaolo had written a letter to the governor in an attempt to have Skindell fired from the casino. DiPaolo emphatically denied the accusation, and went on to explain to the judge that although he and Skindell had an unrelated disagreement several years earlier, there was no such letter. Scozzi not only claimed to have read the letter, but also claimed to have a copy of it, the judge told DiPaolo.

"Why not ask Scozzi for a copy of the letter, telling him you want to confront me with it?" DiPaolo suggested. The judge did exactly that – and now, more than 20 years later, DiPaolo said, the judge is still waiting for the letter.

"It was all a totally false accusation," DiPaolo would later say."These brain trusts should have known that as a privately owned casino, Ed Rendell had absolutely no say-so in who got hired or let go. It was just Foulk and Scozzi attempting to make me look bad."

But DiPaolo in fact did author a letter concerning Skindell. It was in 1996 and addressed to the Erie Police Promotion Board, and it supported

Skindell in his quest to become Deputy Chief – a promotion which Skindell did receive. Later, according to DiPaolo, Skindell stuck it to him, forgetting how DiPaolo helped Skindell's wife get a teaching job in Erie after she moved from Texas to Erie. DiPaolo had been their heroes, he believed, until they no longer needed him.

Another reason – also unfounded – that Foulk might have blamed DiPaolo for Foulk's own shortcomings occurred in 2007 when it was learned Foulk failed to file his re-election financial statement in a timely fashion and in accordance with election laws. Although required to file the statements in the spring, Foulk held off until September 7, months past the deadline.

DiPaolo believed Foulk was trying to hide two financial events from the public.

The first was that Foulk contributed money from his own campaign to Superior Court Judge Michael Joyce, who had been arrested and convicted of insurance fraud and later served prison time.

The second financial incident involved Attorney John Mizner, a local Republican political operative and former Erie County Republican Party Chairman, who enjoyed friendships with both Foulk and Tom Ridge, who contributed to Foulk's campaign, and was found to have misappropriated – stolen, some would say -- $70,000 from his law firm. Foulk refused to prosecute, although the Pennsylvania disciplinary board involving lawyers suspended Mizner's law license for several years.

DiPaolo learned from Erie County Councilman Fiore Leone, Chairman of the Erie County Election Board, that Foulk had approached him directly, claiming that DiPaolo had filed a complaint with the board on Foulk's failure to submit financial documents in a timely fashion. Leone told Foulk there had been no complaint. The law allowed for a $50 fine for every day such reports were late, up to $2,500. Despite being months overdue, Foulk did not pay a single cent in fines. Nor was a complaint filed.

In retrospect, DiPaolo easily pieced together why some law enforcement officials were out to get him – albeit for all the wrong and misleading reasons.

Another indicator that DiPaolo was the real target of the May 2007 contrived federal raid, and not the actual purse lady, occurred on March 2, 2007. That was the day DiPaolo was called by Bob Kuhn, a retired City of Erie Police Officer whom Brad Foulk had hired as a County Detective in the DA's Office.

Previously, DiPaolo had had an excellent working relationship with both Kuhn, and his brother, Norm Kuhn, also an Erie cop. Norm had substance dependence issues when he left the department and had been arrested three times for driving under the influence. Judge DiPaolo offered his help. He had Norm come to his office each morning for eight months to sign in, allowing DiPaolo to physically monitor Kuhn for any indication of alcoholic consumption.

After so many months, Norm Kuhn seemed to be successful in his recovery. Bob Kuhn, DiPaolo recalled, was delighted with DiPaolo for helping his brother with this special personal intervention.

But now, Bob Kuhn, thanks to Foulk, was a member of the Eagle Task Force, which included representatives from the Erie Police Department, Pennsylvania State Police, F.B.I., and also county detectives in Foulk's office. The Eagle Task Force was created to fight the rise of illegal drugs and guns in Erie County.

On the day Bob Kuhn phoned DiPaolo, the judge was in hearings, but as soon as DiPaolo was free, he telephoned the number Kuhn had left for him.

According to DiPaolo, Kuhn said, "I'm at the F.B.I. office. You arraigned a guy named Ammed Abed-Ali and we want you to let him out of jail because he's going to work with us."

DiPaolo recalled he had arraigned the man for another Magistrate, District Magistrate Mack.

"It's officially her case," DiPaolo told Kuhn. "You need to call her with your request."

DiPaolo recalls being surprised that Kuhn became very loud and demanding over the phone, actually yelling, "Are you refusing to help the F.B.I.?"

Hearing how agitated Kuhn was, DiPaolo said, "It's not my call, Bob. It's Judge Mack's. It's her case."

Now, DiPaolo clearly recalls, Kuhn was screaming into the phone: "I DID call her and she said 'No!'"

"Whoa! So you're trying to backdoor her through me?" DiPaolo, now incredulous, said.

"All we want is him out!" Kuhn said.

"Well, sorry, but it's not going to be me that lets him out," DiPaolo begin. But Kuhn said again, "So, you are refusing to help the F.B.I.?"

"Call Mack," DiPaolo said. Kuhn hung up.

Kuhn, who had been Deputy Chief in charge of Traffic Court for the Erie Police Department, was a graduate of the F.B.I. Academy.

He had taken much heat when it was disclosed through a state audit that his personal secretary in that office had embezzled $247,000 from Traffic Court, right under his nose, over a period of years. Kuhn retired shortly after that revelation, and was promptly hired by Foulk.

And now, the incident with Kuhn and his failing plea on behalf of the F.B.I., DiPaolo feels, simply contributed more explosive ammunition for Foulk and Piccinni in the Great Purse Raid just two months later.

CHAPTER 20

POLITICAL PIECES FALL INTO PLACE; THE PITTSBURGH HEAD-HUNTER

The Erie connection aside, the political conspiracy against DiPaolo, a lifelong Democrat, now appeared heading in the direction of an even more significant partisan hit.

Mary Beth Buchanan, the U.S. Attorney for the Western District of Pennsylvania, headquartered in Pittsburgh and Marshall Piccinni's boss, was also a staunch Republican. From what DiPaolo could ascertain, she seemed to have her own very personal agenda and vendetta against the opposing political party; Investigate, jam-up, embarrass, and lock-up Democrats. DiPaolo lost count of the printed news media articles about her head-hunting for Democratic office holders. Articles in the Pittsburgh Post-Gazette and the Pittsburgh Tribune were just the start. The Pennsylvania Progressive, and more. All had the same basic theme: Buchanan "pursuing partisan politics" to scandalize Democrats.

The news media investigation looked at 375 cases handled by Buchanan's office. Of that number, 298 involved Democrats investigated or charged, including former Allegheny County Coroner, Dr. Cyril H. Wecht, a longtime public official who spear-headed national investigations and even was partially responsible for blowing open the NFL's refusal to acknowledge cause and effect in dealing with permanent brain damage from concussions. Of course, Wecht was a lifelong Democrat who once even ran for U.S. Senate in Pennsylvania.

Even more amazing, shocking, actually, was the contents of an article in the Post-Gazette penned by Thomas J. Farrell, an attorney for 18 years who had formerly served as an Assistant U.S. Attorney in Pittsburgh. He called for Buchanan's resignation, citing her own personal agenda. When Buchanan visited Erie, DiPaolo learned, she dined with Piccinni and

Foulk. DiPaolo was also keenly aware of how the Feds operated. Their criminal investigations began with Buchanan giving the okay to her top assistant, who gave the okay to the F.B.I.. Now, DiPaolo had to wonder: Did Buchanan ever attend a purse party?

What's more in adding to her professional reputation being tarnished, in early 2007 the U.S. Senate Judiciary Committee began investigating Buchanan and U.S. Attorney General Alberto Gonzales, Buchanan's boss and President George W. Bush's appointee, for allegedly targeting elected Democratic officials.

All this led DiPaolo to the only reasonable conclusion: He was now convinced that when Piccinni phoned Buchanan, advising her of a Democratic District Judge from Erie who's wife was about to host a purse party in their home, Buchanan was more than pleased to instruct Piccinni to get in there and confiscate those purses – and in the process, not only embarrass DiPaolo, but hit him where it hurt most: targeting his family.

Several years later, Buchanan tossed her hat (and perhaps her purse, who knows!) into the political ring by declaring her candidacy for U.S. Congress in Pittsburgh's congressional district. Republicans felt she would be the front-runner in that race, and she predicted she would raise more than $2 million in support of her candidacy. But on May 17, 2011, Buchanan, who failed to raise anywhere near her predicted war chest, lost her political outing by a landslide.

DiPaolo had long suspected that Buchanan, Piccinni and Foulk got along so well because all were cut from the same soiled fabric.

CHAPTER 21

JUDGE DiPAOLO DOES HIS OWN INVESTIGATION

In the weeks following the raid at his home, DiPaolo began his own private investigation. Recall, however, that he was no novice at probing wrongdoing! He conducted many investigations successfully.

Starting his private probe with the local office of the Federal Bureau of Investigation, Kelly Smith was first on his list, along with his sidekick, Scott Brooks.

As required by law, the Feds were required to provide Defense Attorney Lucas with all "discovery" evidence against his client allowable by the law. Lucas, in turn, provided DiPaolo with all the paperwork relevant to the case. The former cop could only shake his head in disbelief. The material, supposedly compiled by the nation's top law enforcement agency, appeared to DiPaolo to have been gathered and put together by incompetents in a grossly less-than-professional manner.

The two-page "302" document – the Feds' report of their investigation – in which DiPaolo combed through line by line, discusses the interview and interrogation Agents Smith and Brooks conducted with Sharon Lytle. DiPaolo thought back to his rookie days as a cop: In Interrogation 101, cops learn to never question a suspect with others around to overhear the questions and answers. Yet the two federal sleuths talked to Lytle in the presence of both Dominick and Janet DiPaolo as both were seated nearby at their patio table after DiPaolo was called home by his wife.

The second paragraph of the Feds' report actually states that Lytle was advised she would NOT be charged and was not obligated to answer questions. Lie Number One: she was never told any of that – as DiPaolo and his wife could hear everything.

Lie Number Two occurred quickly in the third paragraph, which claimed jewelry and candles were not being sold during the party. In fact, Lytle never told the Feds those objects were not being sold. In fact, they never even asked her about them! It was DiPaolo who informed Piccinni the day after the raid.

By the time DiPaolo got to the fifth paragraph, he would have been laughing if it had been anyone but his own family involved. The report states that Lytle earlier told Janet DiPaolo there would be no invitations or flyers, indicated the women knew it was wrong to hold a purse party. The report also says Lytle would not have approved invitations if she later learned they existed. Lie Number Three: Pure fantasy and fiction, as Lytle never mentioned any of the above to the Feds, nor was she even asked about it.

Lie Number Four sprang up in the eight paragraph. The report claims Lytle said that when the Feds were knocking on the door, Janet told her to hide all the purses in the basement, and she did as she was instructed. The party itself was already in the great room in the basement with 30-plus women in attendance! The great room is 24 feet by 38 feet in size – hardly large enough to do any hiding! Besides, DiPaolo figured, "if what they claimed as true, Lytle would have had to run around carrying and hiding 250 purses while the nitwit feds knocked and knocked."

DiPaolo also found contradictory discrepancies in what the Feds claimed Lytle told them in the sixth and ninth paragraphs.

In one such discrepancy, Lytle is to have said she was "only trying to make a few bucks." But in another, she said she hadn't had many such parties as she was "too busy."

So, DiPaolo opined, the "302" report was laden with lies to cover the Federal agents' appalling behavior – but as DiPaolo continued to examine the documents, it got even better.

For example: The inventory of purses confiscated (see attached) listed:

> On the first day (5-2-07), nine large cargo bags were confiscated which contained 124 purses. A bundle of plastic bags to put the purses in.
>
> On the second day (5-3-07), seven large cargo bags were also confiscated which contained 44 purses.
>
> Total number of purses – 168.

In fact, Janet DiPaolo, after reading the report, recalled that Sharon Lytle had phoned her on Monday, April 30, 2007, just two days before the party, to determine how many invitations Janet had sent out. Lytle needed the approximate number of guests so she could estimate the amount of merchandise she would need to bring to the DiPaolo home. Since Janet was expecting a large gathering, Lytle told her she would bring 250 purses. The importance of this conversation is that is confirmed that Sharon Lytle never told the Feds she cautioned Janet against sending invitations.

Now Janet phoned Sharon after reading the Feds' inventory list and asked how many purses were sold that night. Sharon responded, "Only 10 and some jewelry." Thus, if 250 arrived at the DiPaolo home and 10 were sold, 240 should have been confiscated.

Apparently, the crack Feds forgot that the next day after the party, Judge DiPaolo had carried up the basement stairs from the great room and out of his house seven large cargo bags and turned them over to Agent Uche. Now the Feds had inventoried 168 purses. If 10 were sold, DiPaolo asked himself – where did the missing 72 purses go? Not only were the Feds liars, but are they even worse, he wondered?

DiPaolo recalled that the following day, after phoning Piccinni, the DiPaolo and the agent carried out seven of equal-sized cargo bags that had been in the great room. Nine contained 124 purses; seven held 44. He wondered why, in the Feds' inventory, there was a need for seven bags for just 44 purses. In other words: 124 purses in nine bags, or 13 purses per bag; and 44 purses in six bags, or six per bag. DiPaolo thought, one doesn't have to be well-trained in law enforcement to solve this crime.

"This represented corruption at its worst," DiPaolo said. "And these so-called lawmen arrest those who lie to them? J. Edgar Hoover would have never taken off his dress if he knew these guys from Erie!"

So it now seemed to DiPaolo that the F.B.I.'s local office had little else to keep it occupied; raiding purse parties, and perhaps hoping for bank robberies, which are considered federal offenses. In either case, DiPaolo knew the Feds often were more likely than not to make serious mistakes.

He believes the F.B.I. office in Erie, and the U.S. Attorney's office serving Pittsburgh and Erie, were not actually serving the public, but had instead become a disgrace to the universal principles of law enforcement. Especially when they pull capers like the purse party raid that wastes taxpayer money and embarrasses their families when they are exposed.

He believes the Feds had the pleasure of the Patriot Act in 2005 that was put in place by a young George W. Bush when weapons of mass destruction were nowhere to be found in the Iraq invasion. The U.S.A. Patriot Act was supposed to improve Homeland Security by allowing law enforcement to use tools against drug dealers and organized crime and terrorists, and the use of wiretaps and surveillance of suspected terror-related crimes. Under the act, the Feds could go into a private home with no probable cause, no search warrant, as long as they felt there were terrorism or illegal acts being conducted. Real cops need probable cause.

"Unfortunately, this Patriot Act was being abused by the Rogue Feds, and this purse party was a perfect example of abuse," DiPaolo said.

CHAPTER 22

PARTIES, PARTIES EVERYWHERE; BUT NO F.B.I. RAIDS

In the months following the federal raid on DiPaolo's home in 2007, DiPaolo received many notices and advertising fliers announcing purse parties hosted by hospital auxiliaries, country clubs, businesses, philanthropic and charitable organizations and private homes. DiPaolo, law-abiding citizen and sworn officer of the court, dutifully sent these notices and fliers to the local office of the F.B.I. and copied them to Assistant U.S. Attorney Sanner. Of course, he knew intuitively that nothing would be done. And, surprise of surprises: nothing was.

Yes, despite the many "knock-off" purse parties held in all the days and months after the May 2, 2007, raid on DiPaolo's home, there was not a single federal raid on any of the later events. What's more, there were none before the incident at the DiPaolo home. None before. None after.

It did not take DiPaolo long to understand that the only such raid by the Feds, despite the many parties being held, had already occurred. When knock-offs are sold, everyone knows the items are not the real thing – no one expects to get a $500 purse for $20. The seller is not trying to deceive, and the buyer is not deceived. So – what exactly is the crime? Or the harm? Thousands of golfers buy knock-off Callaways, Titleist, and Taylor-Made clubs, knowing they are not the real merchandise; Foulk had a Callaway, DiPaolo said, remembering their golf outing many years prior.

During the months following the DiPaolo raid, the Feds took a fierce beating on the editorial pages of the Erie Times-News in the Letters-to-the-Editor column. Nearly two dozen letters were written by citizens complaining of the F.B.I.'s actions in the raid. One letter writer suggested that the F.B.I., when not busy hunting purses, could search for the outdoor Christmas decorations that disappeared from his house. Of all the letters, only two were against DiPaolo – one from an office worker DiPaolo had fired years earlier, and another from the mother of a defendant who had appeared in DiPaolo's courtroom and did not like the verdict.

Citizens also voiced their rage with the raid on local radio talk shows and social media.

A year went by without the Feds raiding any other private homes or organizations where purse parties were held and various knock-offs and seconds sold. DiPaolo was starting to believe the Feds must have had a great handle on the counterfeit purse market, and thus had eradicated so called "terrorism" in Erie.

But it wasn't until more than a year after the raid that Attorney Tim Lucas phoned Judge DiPaolo with the news of the indictment, that Assistant U.S. Attorney Christine Sanner officially confirmed to Lucas that Sharon Lytle had been indicted on May 13, 2008, by a Federal Grand Jury on two counts of trafficking in counterfeit goods.

Lucas, quite naturally had asked the federal prosecutor why the indictment took so long – why a year after the fact? Sanner, he said, told him the Feds had been busy with other serious matters and finally had time to prosecute the purse lady. DiPaolo believes it was because of the negative articles in media coverage over the raid. They charged her to save face.

The Erie Times-News was relentless with the story and came out with the front page headline: "Bags Fake – Charges Real". Reporter Ed Palattella went straight for the drama, writing that a unique group of party crashers broke up a gathering at District Judge DiPaolo's home. It was reported, with seeming glee, that the party has since proven to be even more memorable with the Purse Lady being indicted. The five-column newspaper story mentioned Janet DiPaolo's name in the last paragraph, but named Judge DiPaolo twelve (12) times. To the DiPaolos, it was obvious to them that DiPaolo was becoming victim of an organized hatchet job. Most major crimes in the Erie area were investigated by the Erie Police or the Pennsylvania State Police.

"What a liar!" Lucas told DiPaolo, indicating the horrible publicity against the Feds embarrassed them and prompted and pushed them to act against poor Lytle. As the attorney for the defendant – actually, more like the "victim," DiPaolo thought – Lucas provided DiPaolo with copies of all the documents Lucas received from the Feds, as the government was legally mandated to do.

In his 40 years in the criminal justice system, DiPaolo thought nothing new would ever bewilder him. But this indictment – signed by U.S. Attorney Buchanan—did just that – and even more! The Feds had taken photographs of Chanel and Gucci purses. The photos were then sent to Gucci America in New York City. In a letter to the F.B.I. dated April 18, 2008, Gucci store official Jessica Murray said the purse was counterfeit. Ha! There was a revelation!

Another letter, this one from Chanel's Adrienne Sisbarro of New York City, stated that the photo she received from F.B.I. Agent Amamdi on June 7, 2007, depicted a photo of a counterfeit purse. Another bombshell! These two letters were presented to the federal grand jury, which then rubber-stamped the prosecution's case and indicted Lytle.

DiPaolo now suspected that those in the Erie F.B.I. office were so embarrassed by this raid that they used photographs rather than sending the actual purses to the F.B.I. office in New York City so that the purses could be taken directly to the Gucci and Chanel officials for examination. DiPaolo was certain the Erie agents did not want to inform their counterparts in the NYC office of what the Erie office had been up to. The procedure was akin to taking a photograph of a pile of sugar on a table and asking a laboratory to certify that the pile was cocaine.

Not hard to imagine the reaction of agents in New York City, in the midst of their heavy felony case-load – billions of dollars in Ponzi schemes and other white collar crimes, getting innumerable kilos of cocaine off the city streets, dealing with the mob every day – when they opened a box of purses from Erie, Pennsylvania, with a request to have them inspected at the Gucci and Chanel stores. One of Janet DiPaolo's guests, the mother of an out-of-state F.B.I. Agent, phoned her son to inform him she was involved in a raid. He could not stop laughing when he heard the details and said he could not wait to tell his fellow agents the next day.

CHAPTER 23

THE PLOT CONTINUES TO THICKEN: THE FORMER COP TURNED JUDGE REMAINS TENACIOUS

Meanwhile, DiPaolo was meticulous in giving all this new information to Attorney Lucas and an effort to help defend the case against Lytle. But Lucas told DiPaolo that Lytle and her husband merely wanted to get the case over with and move on. They were too frightened by the Feds to fight it!

As a result, on August 13, 2008, the notorious criminal Sharon Lytle, aka "purse lady," entered into the Pre-Trial Diversion Program. Lucas told DiPaolo the Feds offered her admittance into the program to resolve the matter. It resulted in one year of probation. If she served the sentence with no further incidents, the two felony counts would be expunged from her record.

"This is our contribution for a crack-down on counterfeit purses as we address the local crime program," said Andrew Wilson, then in charge of the Erie office of the F.B.I.. In connection with the purse party, he spoke about money laundering by terrorist organizations. DiPaolo thought he had lost his mind. "But yet Piccinni did not want the money from the purse party? DiPaolo questioned?

Since May 2, 2007, and until the publication of this volume 13 years later in 2020, no other home in the City of Erie or Erie County or the entire Commonwealth of Pennsylvania has been raided for a purse party. So much for the federal crackdown on terrorist organizations and money laundering.

Seeking advice on how to best expose the Feds and others over what DiPaolo considered a most-serious miscarriage of justice, over the next

12 months he had numerous conversations with Pennsylvania and U.S. officials – members of the United States Senate, the Superior Court of Pennsylvania, the Judicial Conduct Board of Pennsylvania, and elected representatives of the state legislature, and even with F.B.I. Director Robert S. Mueller's office.

At one point, Judge DiPaolo contacted Pennsylvania's Senior U.S. Senator Arlen Specter. Even though Specter was a Republican, he had earlier expressed some concerns about U.S. Attorney Mary Beth Buchanan's agenda, according to newspaper articles. After many back-and-forth phone calls, Attorney Hannibal Kimerer, Specter's Chief of Staff, gave DiPaolo two options: One, go directly to the news media; and, two, wait until a new U.S. Attorney for Western Pennsylvania is appointed. But the latter depended solely on Barack Obama becoming President.

DiPaolo was also able to confer with U.S. House Judiciary Committee Attorney Eric Tamarakin in Washington, D.C.. Tamarakin gave the judge key information on Attorney Richard Thornburgh, the former Pennsylvania governor and U.S. Attorney General who on October 22, 2007 testified in front of the Judiciary Committee gave damaging testimony against Buchanan. According to the testimony of the Republican Thornburgh, Buchanan was known to target Democratic office-holders. And then, in July 2008, DiPaolo spoke with his longtime friend, Pennsylvania State Representative Pat Harkins, who connected the judge with Attorney Charlie Lyons, Chief of Staff for Pennsylvania U.S. Senator Bob Casey. On Judy 28, Lyons expressed serious interest in the purse raid and the involvement of the U.S. Attorney's Office and the F.B.I..

Ironically, on that same day, MSNBC reported the "breaking news" that Buchanan and U.S. Attorney General Alberto Gonzales who were Republicans, were fired. The gist of the story was that the firings were politically motivated. As a result, Lyons told DiPaolo the Senate Judiciary Committee would be very interested in what appeared to be a pattern of abuse of power by Buchanan and her underlings.

A few days later, on July 31, 2008, DiPaolo and Lyons spoke for more than an hour – the Judiciary Committee was asking DiPaolo to go public with his allegations. But there was a problem: DiPaolo had known from the start that according to Pennsylvania's Judicial Conduct Rules, judges were forbidden from commenting on pending cases – and this case was still open.

On August 8, Lyons phoned DiPaolo with the name of an investigative reporter, Paula Reed-Ward, of the Pittsburgh Post-Gazette. Lyons explained that Reed-Ward has authored a number of uncomplimentary articles on Buchanan. But after DiPaolo contacted the Pennsylvania Judicial Conduct Board, he was strongly advised to re-read the rules before contracting any reporter. In other words, the Board's unofficial response was: Don't do it!

Meanwhile, State Representative Harkins told DiPaolo that perhaps the Pa. House Judiciary Committee could subpoena him, compelling him to testify in front of the committee. That appeared to be in line with the Judicial Conduct Board's rules. But, it was not to be. After meeting with Pa. State Representative Thomas Caltagirone, Chairman of the Judiciary Committee, Caltagirone said the state committee likely did not have the authority to it issue a subpoena in a federal case. The Feds had conducted the raid, not state law enforcement. It was another frustrating strike-out.

But DiPaolo was relentless and determined to push on, despite the setbacks. He conferred with Attorney Thomas Farrell of Pittsburgh, a former U.S. Attorney for Pennsylvania's Western District under President Bill Clinton. Farrell had authored a number of newspaper articles about his successor, advising her to resign for the good of the government. He further advised DiPaolo to go public.

DiPaolo was actually given the phone numbers and e-mail addresses of prominent print and broadcast journalists and commentators such as Eugene Robinson of the Washington Post, Walter Means of the Associated Press, and Nancy Grace and Keith Olbermann. But the judge knew he still could not open up.

Finally, in November 2008, Barack Obama was elected President. A Democratic president at last! Did this change the playing field? Or did it?

DiPaolo still had to wait.

CHAPTER 24

A NEW PRESIDENT - A NEW HOPE! OR NOT?

Politics was in his DNA.

And, as a result, Dominick DiPaolo spent his entire life developing a keen sense of political savvy that would serve him well. Yet, first as a cop and then as a Magisterial Judge, his instinct and sense of morality was to put politics aside. It did not matter if one was Democrat or Republican; what mattered was fairness. Many times he had to be tough, but the toughness never trumped fairness.

That's why it now became so frustrating for DiPaolo to have to depend on politics to achieve fairness for the embarrassment unleashed on his family at the hands of those controlled by political figures.

He kept wondering why, if he could avoid becoming political in his professional law enforcement life, why the F.B.I. and its agents could not? It was a troubling question. But if that's how the federal system now worked, DiPaolo was determined to play by their rules.

Every elected official that Judge DiPaolo spoke with was confident that as soon as a new U.S. Attorney in Pittsburgh was appointed, he or she would be approachable. As the Democrat Obama had succeeded Republican George W. Bush, the new U.S. Attorney in Pittsburgh would undoubtedly be a Democrat. But DiPaolo also knew that if a Republican was appointed, or remained in the position, he could forget justice for his family.

Another complication was the "purse lady."

DiPaolo had three valid reasons that would keep him from taking action before Sharon Lytle had completed her probation.

One, he more than suspected that if he made the issue public, the Feds would interfere with Lytle's light sentence and make life miserable for her and her family. He did not want that to happen. Number two was that the case had to be officially closed before DiPaolo could request and receive all reports of the incident from the F.B.I. and U.S. Attorney under the federal Freedom of Information Act. And finally, he was not yet prepared to make noise and raise red flags in for the feds – quite simply, he did not want to tip his hand.

So, he waited.

CHAPTER 25

JUDGE DiPAOLO GETS HIS TURN AT THE PLATE

Finally! The wait was over.

August, 12, 2009: Sharon Lytle completed her one-year of probation. Less than a month later, on September 2, U.S. District Judge Sean McLaughlin closed out 18-USC 2320 (A) No # -08-22-Erie, F.B.I. #295D-PG-74571.

It was now Judge DiPaolo's turn to treat the feds in the same fashion and malicious way they had treated his wife, family and friends. "Fuck their terrorism bullshit," he thought. "Now it's my turn to break balls, which is never difficult with rats."

Soon, Attorney Julia Dudics-Bagnoni agreed to file the Freedom of Information Act request for the information DiPaolo sought on the case. The federal judge agreed to meet with Dudics-Bagnoni on November 14, 2009, to go over with her the myriad details involved in filing such a request for federal records – daunting at best, and also time-consuming.

With the attorney's caseload and obligations for the upcoming end-of-the-year holidays, she promised DiPaolo that the request for federal records would be filed the first of the year.

Meanwhile, just a few days later on November 19, 2019, Robert Cessar was appointed Interim U.S. Attorney for the Western District of Pennsylvania.

But according to DiPaolo's excellent sources, Cessar was said to be partial to Buchanan, as he was her assistant. DiPaolo knew he could not go directly to him as he was part of the same office and thinking. DiPaolo's frustration grew.

On January 28, 2010. Attorney Dudics-Bagnoni delivered as promised. She wrote a letter to Jeffrey B. Killen, Chief Division Counsel for the F.B.I., and the person who deals with Freedom of Information Act (F.O.I.A.) requests. It took more than a month, but on March 9, 2010, Killen spoke with the Erie attorney and advised her that the request was accepted. Unfortunately since there were many such requests and only 56 Field Units to follow up on them, the time frame for getting the specifics he wanted was between six months and one year.

Again, DiPaolo had to wait.

Almost six months to the day later, on July 26, 2010, DiPaolo finally got what he wanted. Sort of.

In the thick packet sent to Attorney Dudics-Bagnoni, the explanatory letter described 168 pages in the federal investigation stemming from the Great Purse Party Raid. But only 106 pages were released, and many of those were redacted (blacked out). Yet, it was enough for DiPaolo to confirm what he believe was true from the beginning: He had been set up for political reasons.

The federal F.O.I.A. report began with information that had been gathered by the Feds on Rocco and Eileen Marino around August 2005.

The incident number for the Marinos was 295D-PG-74571, the same one used by them for Sharon Lytle. The number was carried over by the Feds as the Marinos are Lytle's parents.

The Federal investigation began back in 2005 when a person (name redacted!) reported (read: snitched to the F.B.I.) that the couple was hosting purse parties in Erie. The report said that the agent (name also redacted!) would prosecute the matter if the allegations proved to be true under Federal Title 18, Section 2320: trafficking in counterfeit goods.

According to the federal report, on November 9, 2005, the Marinos gave a statement to the unnamed agent, saying they purchased the purses from Rice's, 6326 Greenhill Road, New Hope, Pennsylvania. Businesses that also sell the same purses are those in the Millcreek Mall, in kiosks, in Erie's Broad Street Plaza, the Rose Beauty Salon, the Erie Yacht Club, and a business at 901 Route 20 in Ashtabula, Ohio. Attached to the report were sales flyers from Rice's. All of this was included in the report.

On that same date, it was also determined that the U.S. Attorney (no name listed in the report) advised Mrs. Eileen Marino that the case would not be prosecuted, but the F.B.I. would seize the purses.

And so it came to pass that the Feds, in their infinite wisdom and patriotic, anti-terroristic crime-fighting spirit, seized 112 purses – Coach, Gucci, Prada, Kate Spade, Burberry and Coco Chanel; along with 19 wallets – Kate Space, Gucci, Prada, Burberry; and two counterfeit cellular phones from Louis Vuitton; nine Tiffany bracelets and seven Tiffany necklaces.

It would also come to pass that on December 30, 2005, according to the documents, all of the above items were supposedly completely destroyed. And they probably were. At least DiPaolo could find no evidence that Christmas Season of extra pleased Fed wives and/or girlfriends. But now armed with the report of the federal investigation, albeit heavily redacted, Judge DiPaolo restarted his own probe. He learned from Erie Police Detective Rick Marino, nephew of Rocco and Eileen Marino, that his uncle, upset and weeping, telephoned him and indicated the couple was worried they would soon be arrested. Rocco promised Rick they would quit dealing with the knock-offs and never attempt such sales again.

Rick Marino's partner at the time was Lieutenant Maggie Kuhn, who, quite coincidentally, was very good friends with Erie County's "Mr. Law and Order." District Attorney Brad Foulk.

According to Rick Marino's account to DiPaolo, the detective asked Kuhn to intervene on behalf of his aunt and uncle. As a result of such intervention, Marino told DiPaolo that Foulk approached Assistant U.S. Attorney Piccinni and no charges were ever filed against the Marino couple. Of course, they had to give up their source of the merchandise, turn over their inventory, and hold no more purse parties. And that's how the investigation ends.

Marino told DiPaolo he thanked Piccinni and Foulk, to which Foulk cautioned that if they were ever apprehended again, they were on their own. Foulk added that the Feds have other, more important activities to pursue and did not want to be involved in "bullshit like this." At least not until May 2007 at Janet DiPaolo's party.

But time for "bullshit" is exactly what they had!

The report in DiPaolo's possession details an anonymous phone call to the Feds on May 2, 2007 at 2 p.m.

The call told of a purse party that would be held that same day – that very evening, in fact – during which fake purses would be sold. DiPaolo figured it must have been a very slow day in the U.S. Attorney's Office and the Erie Office of the Federal Bureau of Investigation to have such an elite team so suddenly spring into action and within a few hours put together a surveillance team and then a raiding party. But what DiPaolo knew was that that kind of action only happens in 30-minute TV cops shows that include 10 minutes of commercials.

But then DiPaolo recalled that the day after the raid he had phoned Piccinni to advise him of several additional bags of purses that the crack, keenly-observant agents had left behind. During that conversation, Piccinni had said, "If we could have found this woman in her van a few days before, we wouldn't have come to your house, Judge."

But now DiPaolo, as well as any reasonable person, would have to wonder: If the anonymous call about the purses was made on May 2, the day of the raid, how did Piccinni know what woman to look for several days before the raid? And, how did Piccinni and the Feds know which house would be hosting the party on May 2? DiPaolo thought: No integrity, and he can't even lie well.

DiPaolo suspected the entire truth was not being shared that day; his language now, several years later, was slightly stronger.

"As an ex-policeman," he later said, "you sometimes don't give those involved in an explanation all the facts in an effort to get a confession. But what he told me that day was wrong. I mean, c'com, grow some balls. Man up and don't make excuses. Just tell it like it is and don't be a fucking liar!"

And when DiPaolo looked back at the cluster-fuck surveillance on his home, he saw that the hand-written notes by Special Agents Smith and Brooks did not correspond with their official typed report. They certainly were good at setting the stage for these fifty-, sixty- and seventy-year-old female terrorists.

For example, in the agents' hand-written notes, on the day of the raid they have surveillance being launched at 5:35 p.m. At 5:38, they wrote, two women with bags left the house. At 5:34, one woman was reported entering a neighbor's home. Really? Did she have anything to do with criminal activity? Or, perhaps more likely she was returning home from work?

Then, according to the notes, at 5:41, husband leaves in a redacted vehicle. DiPaolo now understand the allegations contained in the notes were totally false, as well as the rundown of women coming and going. DiPaolo, as it turned out, was out of his home before 5:15 p.m. for a 5:30 p.m. meeting at his office. When he left, there was no party in progress and the only woman in his home was his wife, Janet.

"If these rats have photos, they were taken well short of 5:41," DiPaolo would later say. "They apparently were desperate to make it appear that I was home while the party was going on. What rats! In their surveillance notes, they have 40 women entering and leaving. In their typed report, they have 48. They can't even lie straight or reconcile their numbers – I'd hate to have to try to figure out their checking account ledgers!"

Apparently, the surveilling Feds were trying to keep score on how many purses were leaving the DiPaolo home. In the upper right-hand corner of the hand-written notes, the agents were counting bags as the last entry not scratched out was "8 bags."

This would seem to confirm that from 5:35 to 6:31 p.m., some eight to 10 purses were sold; exactly as Sharon Lytle had advised them. It might have been the only fact the Feds had right. Recall that Vicki Fabrizio had left her purchased purse at the house.

DiPaolo also learned that at some point during the one-hour fiasco, Rocco and Eileen Marino, Sharon's parents, arrived and the house to meet with Sharon about two purses that had been previous purchased that were apparently flawed.

As the Marinos left the home with the purses, either Agent Smith or Agent Brooks must have been familiar with them from the 2005 investigation and stopped them. According to the federal report, a receipt was given to them for the two purses, one bearing the Coach name and the other Kate Spade, and the Marinos were allowed to proceed on their way.

Even though he knew the Marinos were gone and hadn't returned to the house, when Smith entered the home he none-the-less asked Janet DiPaolo if the Marinos were there. Smith also told Janet DiPaolo that Sharon Lytle was warned back in 2005 not to be involved in purse parties. But in the 302 Form from 2005, only Rocco and Eileen Marino were investigated and interviewed. The Feds apparently never spoke with or warned Lytle. Another lie? Lytle's name never appeared in the report.

"They will often tell those they interview: 'You lie to the F.B.I., you go to jail,'" DiPaolo later said. "Yet these Feds hardly ever tell the truth – to anyone. No law enforcement officers should ever lie in their reports. Just tell it like it is." Rogue cops do these illegal things.

Also attached to the F.O.I.A. document were three separate reports indicating that two purses were confiscated from the Marinos, 124 purses of various brands overall were taken on May 2, 2007, and another 44 purses of various brands confiscated on May 3, 2007. All the purses were supposedly destroyed on September 16, 2009, seven days after Judge McLaughlin closed the case. DiPaolo wondered who witnessed the destruction. The purses on May 3rd were turned over not confiscated. Get it right.

According to DiPaolo calculations, it appears that at least 72 purses were not listed or accounted for in the final inventory and destruction.

From the Freedom of Information Act documents, DiPaolo read that the agents contacted a woman and requested that she identify the purses as counterfeit. But the woman told them she did not have the expertise to determine the difference between authentic and fake merchandise, but said she would assist the agents in directly contacting purse manufacturers Gucci, Dolce and Gabbana, Chanel, Coach and Kate Spade.

"Going to someone lacking expertise for expert information?" DiPaolo asked. "Just what kind of a non-professional investigation was this? Perhaps the woman they sought out was the wife of local F.B.I. Agent, Jerry Clark – she certainly had some experience with fake purses."

But it wasn't until April of 2008, 11 months later, that the Feds sent photos of the purses to Chanel, Gucci, Liz Claiborne, Kate Spade and Juicy Couture. According F.O.I.A. documents, the purse images were sent by e-mail.

And finally, on May 13, 2008, after receiving their e-mail confirmation that the purses were fake, the raiders took their information to a Federal Grand Jury, eventually getting Sharon Lytle indicted on two counts of violating Title 18-Section 2320, Trafficking in Counterfeit Goods.

The F.O.I.A. report also indicated that an "assisting agency" was involved in the investigation, but the agency's name was redacted. As DiPaolo thought of the possibilities – Erie Police, Pennsylvania State Police, Pennsylvania Attorney General or Erie County District Attorney's Office, only one made sense for the Feds to avoid giving up – Piccinni's best pal, Brad Foulk, who DiPaolo was believed to be a the dirty D.A.

And DiPaolo was willing to bet his house that he knew who the identity of the redacted assisting rat.

On August 12, 2008, United States Attorney for the Western District of Pennsylvania Mary Beth Buchanan accepted and authorized Sharon Lytle to be placed in the federal Pre-trial Diversion Program. According to Form 302, her case was to be placed in an inactive status as there were no investigative leads to pursue

"It clearly shows without a doubt that the Feds did not really care about where the purses were coming from or who was distributing them in quantity," DiPaolo later said. "So much for their high and mighty lofty claims of fighting acts of terrorism.

A year later, on August 12, 2009, Lytle's federal probation was over. During the entire 12-month period, no federal agent asked her a single question about counterfeit purses, or who else had hosted parties. She was not asked about those involved in law enforcement hosting parties. Nothing.

In reality, the F.O.I.A. revealed, or confirmed, much of what DiPaolo already knew from the beginning. For one, there was no anonymous caller – but there was an "assisting agency," one that the Feds did not want to expose. This also serves to confirm Agent Brooks' earlier statement to Airport Chief Bagnoni about District Attorney Brad Foulk and Marshall Piccinni.

What's more, the missing evidence is pretty much confirmed by the surveillance count of the purses purchased. And the prior investigation with the Marinos two years earlier, the one that Foulk quietly killed, all add up to a huge conspiracy directed entirely at DiPaolo. Even more: Why would the Feds wait a year before taking action against Lytle, and why did they operate in such a clumsy way in regard to not confiscating the money and how the purses were ID'd in such an unprofessional way.

But most important to DiPaolo – the biggest red flag or "smoking purse" – was why the Feds never stopped the sales at the warehousing level. They just appeared to go through the motions to make their effort look efficient by indicting Sharon Lytle while saving face in the eyes of the citizens of Erie.

After going through this new and confirming information in July 2010, DiPaolo was anxious to make his move to expose who he believe to be the conspirators and co-conspirators. But there still wasn't a new and permanent U.S. Attorney named for the Western District of Pennsylvania.

So, instead of going public in a major way, Judge DiPaolo met again with Attorney Dudics-Bagnoni and decided to file an appeal with the Feds in an attempt to retrieve the redacted information under the Freedom of Information Act.

Yet, a short time later, DiPaolo was notified that David Hickton had been confirmed as U.S. Attorney for the Western District of Pennsylvania in Pittsburgh, with jurisdiction over Erie.

Hickton, then 54, was said to be a sharp lawyer, originally from Columbus, Ohio, but educated at Pennsylvania colleges, getting his J.D. degree from the University of Pittsburgh School of Law. So, he was extremely familiar with Western Pennsylvania.

Pittsburgh Attorney Kevin Colosimo, a mutual friend and professional acquaintance of both DiPaolo and Hickton, told DiPaolo he would speak to Hickton about getting together with the Erie magisterial judge to discuss DiPaolo's concerns. But Colosimo suggested they wait until Hickton became more firmly established and comfortable in his new position, since the new U.S. Attorney wasn't to be officially sworn into office until August 12, 2012.

DiPaolo had kept Colosimo informed about the case since the 2007 purse party raid.

In fact, DiPaolo had discussed with the attorney the possible filing of a Bivens Action against the Feds for illegal search and seizure, as well as violation of the DiPaolos' Constitutional rights.

But since neither DiPaolo nor his wife, Janet, had been charged, and with the judge giving consent by telling Janet to allow the Feds to enter their home and voluntarily surrendering the purses, it appeared there was no real legal standing to file a Bivens Action.

However, that did not keep DiPaolo, still as tenacious as he always had been, from moving forward with his appeal of the redacted federal information. On September 14, 2010, Attorney Dudics-Bagnoni sent the Letter of Appeal to the Feds, requesting the disclosure of the outside "assisting agency." Less than two weeks later, the attorney received a letter confirming receipt of the appeal.

About the same time, DiPaolo got word from his Pittsburgh contract, Colosimo that Hickton requested that DiPaolo send him an official letter to begin the review process at the U.S. Attorney's level. DiPaolo was eager to comply, but first wanted to wait for results of the appeal so he could provide that information as well to Hickton.

Another wait!

Three months passed and still no action, either way, on the F.O.I.A. redacted appeal. So, on December 6, 2010, DiPaolo sent a four-page, single-spaced letter to Hickton outlining the details of the purse raid more than three years earlier, and the actions taken at that time by Hickton's predecessor and by the Erie office of the Federal Bureau of Investigation.

Hickton wrote back on December 17, advising that his office would reach out to Judge DiPaolo by the first of 2011 to discuss the concerns raised in his letter of December 6.

While DiPaolo was encouraged by Hickton's interest in the case, the judge was disappointed to learn that on December 20, 2010, Attorney Dudics-Bagnoni was notified that the Feds refused to identify the third party – the "assisting agency" – that helped the Feds with the purse raid. The Feds claimed the request was an unwarranted invasion of the personal privacy of the third party. Basically, the response was: If you don't like it, file a lawsuit under 5 USC 552 (A) (4) (B); an appeal to obtain the requested information in the reports. While disappointed, it came as no surprise. DiPaolo knew there would be a smart-ass response with the denial of the appeal.

DiPaolo was tempted to ask Dudics-Bagnoni write back to the Feds, advising that they knew actually who the assisting agency was – it was District Attorney Brad Foulk – and since Foulk had died August 13, 2009, it was no longer an invasion of personal privacy to identify a dead person. In fact, Foulk's buddies, including Piccinni, Cunningham and Pennsylvania Attorney General Tom Corbett, later the governor, were among the pallbearers.

DiPaolo knew from the start that it was Foulk who was helping the Feds. DiPaolo knew that Foulk had always had a big mouth. He blabbed a lot when he should have stayed silent on a lot of things.

As DiPaolo put it together, Foulk gave himself up not once, but twice. The first time was when he acknowledged to Vicki Fabrizio that he learned of the raid on the day of the event, hours before the raid took place. Most of those involved in law enforcement know that no one talks of a raid with an agency outsider before the fact.

So, Foulk was not an outsider after all.

Secondly, all that Fabrizio incorrectly told Foulk about thinking that Janet DiPaolo would deliver the purses over the weekend, was repeated by Foulk to the newspaper reporter Palattella and retold the bogus information word for word to Attorney Logue.

And remember lying Foulk when he told Vicki Fabrizio that he learned of it on May 2, 2007 at 1 p.m. The 302 Report states the Feds received an anonymous call about a party at 2 p.m. That's what happens when you lie, you get caught. Foulk and Piccinni both thought they were slick with their stories, not realizing they would get caught when DiPaolo put it together.

CHAPTER 26

MEETING WITH THE FEDS: ANOTHER SET UP!

A woman who identified herself as "Kathy" from U.S. Attorney Hickton's Office, phoned DiPaolo to set up the long-awaited meeting and DiPaolo's first real opportunity to seek justice for what he believe to be political retribution and for the embarrassment caused his family. Hickton wanted to meet with DiPaolo in Pittsburgh in late February, and offered several days.

But a number of events ranging from surgery in his family to a primary election fight during that late winter and early spring resulted in a series of delays, of scheduling and rescheduling the Hickton meeting.

Finally in late May, after several more months of back-and-forth phone calls between DiPaolo and "Kathy," a date was agreed upon by both parties and set for 10:30 a.m. on Wednesday, June 29.

DiPaolo and Attorney Tony Logue, a good friend and legal advisor, who had unrelated business in Pittsburgh that day, drove the 125 miles to the U.S. Attorney's Office on June 29, arriving there at 10:05 a.m. for the long-anticipated 10:30 meeting.

They checked in at the front desk, were given Visitor Passes, then waited in the lobby until 10:35 when a woman, who did not introduce herself, but whose voice DiPaolo recognized as "Kathy," led them to a conference room where Hickton and several others were gathered. DiPaolo, who had been in the lobby more than 35 minutes with no others coming or going, immediately sensed that this group had been in the Conference Room at least that long and possibly longer.

Whether or not they had been discussing DiPaolo's letter of the previous December or other federal business was not known – but it would later appear likely to DiPaolo that he was the main topic of the group's concern.

Once inside the conference room, Hickton introduced himself, along with a woman he identified as his first assistant. Also present was another woman, whom Hickton said was with the F.B.I., a male from the U.S. Attorney's Office, and a man identified as Leo Dillon, a lawyer with Hickton's office.

DiPaolo and Logue immediately passed around their business cards to all present, but did not receive any such cards in return. DiPaolo was surprised. At every business meeting he had ever attended, cards were always exchanged so everyone present knew with whom they were dealing. But now, the simple element of this one-sided cards distribution not only seemed strange, but also seemed to set the tone for what was to come.

Everyone sat down in their assigned seats and then…Silence. No one was saying anything. After a few minutes in such an uncomfortable environment, DiPaolo finally spoke up, telling Hickton how much he appreciated the U.S. Attorney taking the time to meet with him.

"I'm not here to get anyone in trouble, or to have anyone disciplined," DiPaolo began, "but only to advise you about what happened to my family so it doesn't happen to anyone else in Erie."

No response from Hickton. No response from anyone in the room. But then, within minutes, DiPaolo began to think he had been set-up. Not again!

He immediately recognized that an interrogation was beginning. After all, he had been a cop for 25 years, most of that time a homicide detective. He knew all the tricks of trade and it was quickly apparent to him that his letter and concerns were not only discussed among themselves, but also with Assistant U.S. Attorney Piccinni.

No one present in the room appeared concerned about any Fed who might have been guilty of a wrongdoing; or even if someone had done anything wrong, they did not seem to care.

Attorney Dillon did most of the talking. He had excerpts from DiPaolo's December letter highlighted on different pages. DiPaolo wasn't impressed with his style. "If this is the best they have to conduct an interview or interrogation, then they are in trouble," he thought.

"Why did you say this is the worse abuse of office one can imagine?" the questions began.

"How do you know Attorney Piccinni was present? He didn't enter your home?"

"How is this a political payback?"

"How do you know Attorney Piccinni told the news media?"

"How do you know Mary Beth Buchanan had anything to do with this?"

"Did you itemize the so-called missing evidence?

"Who told you Attorney Piccinni wants to run for Judge?"

"Why did you copy this letter to all the heavy hitters?"

DiPaolo attempted to answer each of the questions, but each answer appeared to draw an argument from Dillon. They were not the answers, it seemed to DiPaolo, that Dillon wanted to hear. Every question was about their boy Piccinni.

But when DiPaolo brought up the information about Agent Jerry Clark's wife hosting a purse party, there was stone, icy silence. Nothing like, "How do you know that?" Or, "Who told you?" Or, "Do you know anyone who supposedly was present?" Zip. Nada. No questions.

The same silence occurred when DiPaolo told the group that the "Purse Lady" was willing to give up her source of the so-called counterfeit purses, but the local federal law enforcement authorities were simply not interested. Again, not a single inquiry of how DiPaolo had obtained such disturbing information. And both of these issues were in DiPaolo's letter.

But then, when DiPaolo casually alleged that the F.B.I. Agents involved in the May 2007 raid had lied in the 302 report, every member of the group stiffened and almost in unison demanded: "Where did you get the 302?"

"Amazing!" DiPaolo thought. Here they apparently had been waiting to ambush DiPaolo since the previous December, and yet not one of them had checked into whether the Judge had filed for the report under the Federal Freedom of Information Act. "Shame on them!" DiPaolo thought to himself, slowly shaking his head. "These guys are even more fucking stupid than I thought!"

And now, as DiPaolo told the group he had filed for and received the report on the F.O.I.A., they all seemed to look at one another in a confused state.

"Typical Feds," DiPaolo thought. "No preparation. Clueless. No wonder they get no respect."

Finally, the U.S. Attorney for the Western District of Pennsylvania, who until now had remained mostly silent, spoke:

Hickton: "Did your wife send out invitations (to the purse party)?"

DiPaolo: "Yes. To her family and friends."

Hickton: "Did she use your letterhead from court?"

The quick answer was, "Of course not." Hickton then stood, said he had another meeting, and left the room.

But then DiPaolo had to wonder again about the gross lack of efficiency of the office that surprised even him. He recalled that during the raid, agents were stopping women outside his home and asking them if they were sent invitations. The agents wanted to know if any of the women actually had brought the invitations with them. Of course, nobody did. Who would?

One young woman told the agents she might have the invitation at her home. And at 10 p.m., three hours after the raid, Agent Smith appeared at the woman's house asking if she had found the invitation. She hadn't. But she did phone Janet DiPaolo the next morning to inform her of the visit.

And then Smith asked, "What kind of paper was it on?"

"Paper?" the woman replied to the weird question. "Just regular paper. White paper." Of course, no judicial/court letterhead. "Just a computer-generated invitation."

It all began to fit in for Judge DiPaolo. This was no longer about terrorists. Or counterfeit purses. Or purse parties. It was about Judge DiPaolo. Judge DiPaolo the Democrat.

DiPaolo thought to himself that over the years he, along with Erie County Councilman Fiore Leone and State Representative Flo Fabrizio held family Christmas parties, attending by more than 1,000 invitees, at various school gyms.

These parties were funded personally by the elected officials from Erie's Sixth Ward – and none of the three ever used their official office letterheads on the invitations. Janet DiPaolo had invited her family members, including aunts and cousins, as well as her personal friends to the purse party. Why would she even think to use her husband's letterhead on the invitations?

As DiPaolo's thought process continued, he believed Hickton and his Fed counterparts to be incompetent to even make such ridiculous assumptions and getting paid exorbitant salaries.

"What a rip-off of the public," DiPaolo thought.

Hickton later left the U.S. Attorney's office for a position with the University of Pittsburgh.

"I hope they're not counting on his expert investigative techniques," DiPaolo later said.

And now, DiPaolo had to involuntarily shake his head over the further example of amateur police work. When Agent Smith was at the DiPaolo house during the raid, why didn't he simply ask Janet DiPaolo for an invitation to examine? Because, DiPaolo thought, the Feds were going to lie on their 302 and say the purse lady told Janet not to send invitations – which the lady never said.

As DiPaolo sat there with Hickton and the others, he thought of the file folder he had brought along with him. Included in it were his notes, documents, and F.B.I. reports. Also in the folder was a pristine invitation to the now infamous purse party, an invitation created by Janet DiPaolo's computer, and most certainly not on judicial letterhead!

For a brief second or two, he was about to reach into the folder and produce the invitation that the Feds were so interested in exposing. But now he knew that these people were not at all concerned with his accusations, and even the meeting appeared to be a ruse. Reveal the invitation to them? Bullshit!

Now, DiPaolo wondered whether Attorney Colosimo was involved. The attorney had told DiPaolo he had once represented Hickton in a legal matter, but didn't specify what the legal matter was. And, Hickton's appointment as U.S. Attorney had seemed to take a long time to DiPaolo –had there been skeletons in his closet that delayed the appointment? DiPaolo did not know. But after the meeting, Colosimo never spoke to DiPaolo again.

When a Judge gives his instructions to a jury, prior to deliberations he advises. "False in One, False in All (Falsus in Uno, Falsus in Omnibus is the expression). This is pointed out to juries when evidence and testimony is in question. It means that if juries find that a witness has lied under oath, the jury has the right to believe all the testimony was false. "This fits this case to a tee," DiPaolo said.

CHAPTER 27

THE SET-UP BECOMES CLEAR; MORE LIES THAN DONALD TRUMP!

Still fuming during this one-sided and obviously biased meeting with the Feds, where it was becoming more and more evident that DiPaolo was being set-up, the Judge thought back to day following the wrongful purse raid when he spoke with Piccinni about the seven full bags of purses that had been left behind in the DiPaolo home.

"Did your wife send invitations?" Piccinni asked DiPaolo with what now appears to have been feigned innocence.

"Yes, of course," DiPaolo had replied, wondering to himself how Piccinni figured all those women got there.

But Piccinni responded with, "Last night, she told the agents she did not send them."

DiPaolo, however, did not hesitate and said, "Look, I was there with her the entire time while your agents were at our home and I never heard her being asked about invitations. Never." Why would she lie?

No response from Piccinni.

And now DiPaolo also recalled that when he told Piccinni that he knew the federal attorney was at his home, Piccinni hesitated before replying, "Oh, yeah. I dropped my kid off for soccer practice, so I was in the area."

But DiPaolo knew that Piccinni's son played soccer for his school in Edinboro, at least 15 miles from DiPaolo's home. Another lie on top of the lie about Janet DiPaolo being asked about sending out invitations.

And now in this Pittsburgh federal prosecutor's office, just from the very nature of the questions being asked by Dillon, it was clear to DiPaolo that this lawyer had been briefed by the Erie agents or Piccinni or both. Sadly, he was now convinced that his 125 mile trip to Pittsburgh was a monumental waste of his time. Nowhere in the "302" by Smith and Brooks did it say they asked Janet about sending invitations or her responding "no."

A year earlier, on July 29, 2010, DiPaolo recalled, F.B.I. Director Robert Mueller commented in a news article about the scandal involving F.B.I. Agents caught cheating on their promotion tests. Mueller, at the time, said the embarrassment raised questions about whether the F.B.I. even knows its own rules for conducting investigations on Americans. How true, DiPaolo thought. And sad.

"For what these rats did on May 2, 2007," DiPaolo thought, "his comments hit the nail directly on the head."

And now, with the pieces of this puzzle falling into place, it became apparent to DiPaolo that whoever tipped off Foulk and the Feds about Janet DiPaolo's party had lied by giving the alleged crime fighters bogus information, falsely claiming that the invitations were sent out on DiPaolo's official letterhead, and DiPaolo knew from the get go who the person was.

One of the purse party guests, Erie businesswoman Daria Reymore, who owned Office Machine Sales and Service with her husband, Larry, later told DiPaolo that Mike Morrocco, a wannabe politician, asked her if she attended. Morrocco knew of Daria's relationship with the DiPaolos and wanted to see her invitation.

Daria wanted to know why he would want the invitation, and Morrocco asked if she could get an invitation "with DiPaolo's letterhead for Brad." But Reymore was aghast!

"What's wrong with you people!" she said. "The invitation was from Janet. It wasn't on Dom's letterhead and Dom had nothing to do with it."

Morrocco, who owns a rundown garage in Erie's Little Italy neighborhood, had earlier contracted with former Erie Mayor Louis Tullio to tow cars for the police department, those illegally parked, in accidents or simply abandoned. It is believed by some that Tullio personally financially benefited from the city doing contract business with those like Morrocco.

When DiPaolo was an Erie police Detective Sergeant in the 1980s, he had arrested Morrocco after he towed an off-duty cop's car. Morrocco lied to the cop, denying knowing anything about the car, but applied to the state for a title stating the car was being junked. Shortly after that, the cop with the missing car, Sergeant David Grassi, saw his car going down the street. He quickly stopped the driver, who said he bought the car from Morrocco. Ironically, Grassi was the nephew of Mayor Tullio! DiPaolo charged Morrocco with failure to make required disposition of funds or property received, and unauthorized use of a motor vehicle. As one might expect, the city relieved Morrocco of his lucrative towing gig. Grassi did not show at the hearing, allegedly acting at the request of his mayoral uncle, "Big Lou." Grassi told DiPaolo, "He lost his towing contract, so forget about it."

Morrocco, and his buddy Mike DeDad, aka "Whispers," were very close to DA Brad Foulk. DeDad, Erie's Third Ward Democratic Chairman, serving the Little Italy area, was a significant supporter of the Republican Foulk. DeDad went as far as holding fundraisers for Foulk at La Nuova Aurora Club, run by DeDad and his brother, Tony. DiPaolo believed DeDad saw himself as a legend in Erie politics, but when he ran for District Judge in his own home Third Ward, he could not get even 100 votes out of the hundreds cast. For Democratic Party leaders to openly support a Republican such as Foulk was considered a most severe political no-no, but they did it quite openly failing to learn. DiPaolo knows, that Foulk used them for his own advantage, just as he used others because of his position.

"No Rhodes Scholars in that bunch," DiPaolo often thought.

All this talk of who sent the invitations irritated DiPaolo to no end! All who knew him were aware he served in office by the book – never using his position for personal gain or to the advantage of his family. Apparently the feds were having a difficult time dealing with and understanding someone with scruples who abides by the ethics of his office. And why would Janet send an invitation to her aunts, cousins and close friends on her husbands letterhead. That makes no sense.

DiPaolo, while thinking about this entire fiasco and poor Lytle being charged, put on probation and paying with her reputation only because "these rats wanted to strike back at me," was appalled at a corrupt system he had worked all his life to keep honorable. He thought of the F.B.I.'s Jerry Clark and his wife wife's purse party. He thought of Cindy DeSantis, wife of Joe DeSantis, Secret Service Agent body guard for former Pennsylvania Congressman, Governor and U.S. Homeland Security Secretary Tom Ridge, holding her own purse party at their Fairview, Pa., home, and Joe and other agents carrying the purses from Sharon's van into the house. But somehow the Feds did not consider that as domestic terrorism. For the Feds like Clark and Piccinni, the rules appeared to be different. A confidential source also tipped off DiPaolo that a day before the DiPaolo purse party raid, Piccinni and the Feds called Scott Curtis, an Internal Revenue Service agent stationed in Erie, and asked that he accompany them on the raid to make it appear the IRS was also involved.

"I don't know Curtis, but he must have a lot of integrity," DiPaolo later said. "He refused Piccinni's invitation, knowing the entire premise was bullshit."

After this internally pensive, but brief moment during the Pittsburgh meeting, DiPaolo turned to his friend, Attorney Tony Logue, and said, "Let's go. This was nothing but a big waste of time."

As they rose to leave, Dillon was still sputtering, saying, "But I'm not done yet! I still want to ask you about Unicredit. That Ed Palattella is really on you about this!" But DiPaolo held his tongue. But not his thoughts: Those mother fuckers! "I am," DiPaolo replied. And they walked out, leaving the most of the others in the room with mouths agape. DiPaolo was well aware of the "thin blue line" in law enforcement, the unwritten rule that cops should always stick together. But this abuse of power, especially by a federal attorney and F.B.I. personnel, was mind-boggling to the former cop DiPaolo.

As they got into their car, DiPaolo knew he had made a huge mistake by writing and sending the letter to the Feds with the hope that someone in the new administration would listen. He and Logue could not believe the Feds actually brought up Unicredit. They apparently were ready for DiPaolo with a double-barrel – but had no ammo in it. It was unloaded.

Attorney Logue made his one o'clock appointment at the District Attorney's Office, and shortly after they drove home.

But now he knew that Democrat, Republican or Independent, political affiliation did not matter – they were all Feds and right or wrong, especially when they are wrong, they all stick together. They were so fixated on destroying Judge DiPaolo that they violated every rule, law and moral obligation, DiPaolo believed. "Law enforcement officers take oaths to uphold the Constitution, including Piccinni and the F.B.I.," he said.

Some might wonder what drives DiPaolo along this path. After all, the case is basically over. No one got badly hurt or went to jail. Life moves on.

But Dominick DiPaolo learned many years ago that history shows us that when good people do not stand up to an injustice, that injustice will slowly continue to pick apart the core of our society.

No Don Quixote of La Mancha fame, who charged at windmills, DiPaolo the realist former cop and now District Judge, vowed to fight on, no matter how long it took or how far he had to go. He knew he must continue this battle, not only for himself, but also for his wife and family; and for the good people of Erie, Pennsylvania.

MAGISTERIAL DISTRICT COURT 06-1-05
ERIE COUNTY, PENNSYLVANIA

DOMINICK D. DiPaolo
DISTRICT JUDGE

1563 WEST 38TH STREET
ERIE, PA 16508
TELEPHONE: (814) 451-6520
FAX: (814) 451-6514

December 6, 2010

United States Attorney Office
David J. Hickton, United States Attorney
United States Court House
700 Grant Street, Suite 4000
Pittsburgh, Pennsylvania 15219

Dear U.S. Attorney Hickton;

Initially, let me congratulate you on your confirmation as United States Attorney for the Western District of Pennsylvania. I am sure you and your family are quite proud of this wonderful accomplishment.

I write this letter on the advice of my attorney, Kevin Colisimo, who advised this procedure as the appropriate manner in which to explain my concerns with some past conduct with your office here in the Erie Division. Before specifically addressing those concerns, please let me briefly identify myself.

Since 1994, I have served as the elected Magisterial District Judge, 06-1-05, in the six Ward City of Erie. In 2012 I will finish up my third, six-year term. I am a registered Democrat but have won nomination on both the Democratic and Republican tickets each time I have run. Before taking the oath as judge, I was City of Erie Policeman, serving for twenty-five years. Twenty-four of those years were as a Detective Sergeant. I was involved in thousands of investigations and arrests. I was the lead investigator in over 30 homicide cases.

During that time, I was assigned as a Special Investigator with the Federal Grand Jury to work with the Assistant United States Attorney in Erie. I also served as a Special Agent with the Pennsylvania Office of Attorney General to work one of its grand jury investigations. In 1994, I was honored by the Erie City

Council as the "Most Decorated Police Officer" in the history of the Erie Police Department. In 2004, I was appointed by Governor Ed Rendell, as a Commissioner, with the Pennsylvania Commission on Crime and Delinquency. As you probably are aware, this Commission draws its membership from the courts and all the top law enforcement agencies in the Commonwealth including the prisons and probation. I was the only Magisterial District Judge to ever sit on the board, which awards over seventy-million dollars to a variety of organizations in the Criminal Justice system.

My concerns about your Erie Division Office don't arise out of any of the foregoing, but an event that took place on May 2, 2007, in which I experienced the worst abuse of power one could imagine. The Justice System in this Commonwealth and in this Country is the greatest system in the world, when people of integrity and honesty participate. Unfortunately, on that night and the following days and months, the system failed because of dishonest and deceitful conduct of people who participate and are in charge of it in their capacities as employees of the Federal Government.

My sixty-year old wife, Janet, hosted a "Spring Party" with a group of her friends and relatives in our home, like thousands of women routinely do in their homes across this Commonwealth and Country. The mother of an F.B.I. agent (out of state), private and public-school administrators, the wife of a Pennsylvania State Legislator, high ranking administrators in law enforcement, and a number of professional women, who are well respected in our Community, as well as housewives, mothers, and grandmothers attended this party. That night, the reason for their attendance and central attraction to the event, was the discount sale of purses, jewelry, key chains, and sun glasses by the woman conducting the sale. But Assistant United States Attorney Marshall Piccinini, from the Erie Office accompanied by five F.B.I. Agents, decided to conduct a raid on my home for what they claim were "knock-off" counterfeit purses being sold.

There is no doubt that the purpose of conducting this raid, and all the accompanying news articles chronicling the event, was not done with the intent to begin a campaign to stop counterfeiting and the illegal sale of "knock off" goods. Rather, the sole purpose of the raid was to embarrass me, for "political pay-backs" and for other reasons. At the time of the event and subsequent raid, I was working at my judicial office. This raid occurred at 7:00PM. The federal agents were gone by 7:15PM. The manner in which the entire event was prepared for and conducted is another story. Investigations 101 were violated start to finish.

The Federal Court House in Erie opens at 8:00AM for the public. At 7:05AM the next morning, a newspaper reporter who covers the Federal Courthouse beat ran into an Erie Attorney at a coffee shop and advised him that "Judge DiPaolo's home was raided by F.B.I. last night." This is just one item of proof supporting my belief that AUSA Piccinini had but one thing in mind; to embarrass me by calling the media before the courthouse was even open.

Before he was appointed to handle your Erie Division Office, Republican Erie County District Attorney, Brad Foulk, employed Republican, Marshall Piccinini as an ADA. At the time of the "raid," Republican, Mary Beth Buchanan, was "calling the shots" in your office. You obviously are already aware what her agenda was. It was well known around the Erie law enforcement community that Foulk was upset with me since I received the appointment to the PCCD that he wanted and had been trying to obtain. Furthermore, he was upset with me for criticizing him on an investigation his office was conducting, in which I requested financial records from Erie County, which indicated he took political contributions from the targets of the investigation when it was being conducted.

In its initial report of the "purse party raid," the F.B.I. states that on May 2, 2007, they received an "anonymous" call in regards to the party. Piccinini told me a few days after the raid that they (the Feds) attempted but were unable to find the "purse lady" conducting the event a couple days before the party and had they been successful, my wife would not have been involved. They cannot even lie right.

One of the F.B.I. Agents who was present at my home during the raid, advised a high ranking law enforcement officer after the raid that F.B.I did not want to participate but "Marshall (Piccinini) and Brad (Foulk) wanted it done to embarrass DiPaolo." Another F.B.I. Agent, who did not participate at this miscarriage of justice in my home, why as his wife hosted a purse party just a few months earlier, therefore he thought it best to "stay away." Apparently, the Feds must have given themselves immunity.

I can go on and on about the "missing" evidence that was seized and not reported, which only the investigators from your Erie Office know what happened to, and how these missing items were allegedly determined to be counterfeit. But that can wait for a later time. The purpose of this letter is to alert you about how things operate in your Erie Office and what you have here. I realize Piccinini is a career prosecutor and the only way he leaves office is if he retires, or runs for judge as he is now apparently discussing with those outside his inner circle. But is abuse of the power of his office and selective prosecutorial enforcement needs to cease. Hopefully, now that we have a new U.S. Attorney in office, the end of that process can begin in earnest.

With all the negative publicity the local, federal prosecutorial offices received over this egregious act, a year later they charged the "purse lady," obviously with the sole purpose in mind of justifying the raid. She entered into a pretrial diversion agreement and through her attorney, agreed to provide information as to the identity and location of the "retailers" who sold these purses in and out of Erie County. Despite being prepared to provide the necessary information, she ultimately was also told by Piccinini's people that it was "not necessary" and that she should simply cease conducting the parties in the future. Does this type of response sound like a "crackdown" by the Feds on the sale and distribution of counterfeit items as they want the public to believe?

On May 15, 2008, Andrew Wilson, head of the F.B.I. in Erie, said in an interview to his source at the Erie Times that this was "our contribution to a crackdown on the sale of counterfeit purses as we address local crime through counterfeiting and terrorist organizations." Since this "raid" not one other home in the Commonwealth has been visited by the Feds, State or local police for purposes of stopping a purse party. Purse parties continue to thrive in Erie, at clubs, non-profit organizations, and in private homes. The local U.S. Attorney Office and F.B.I. agents working out of it have been given brochures and fliers identifying where these parties are being held and allegedly counterfeit purse being sold, yet apparently there is absolutely no interest in interfering with them now that the raid on my home has taken place. It is also confirmed that Secret Service Agents at one Erie County home were present when a purse party was held.

At this time, I would like the opportunity to personally meet with you and fully discuss this matter. There are many other things you need and should be aware of. Despite its recent success in a legitimate, high profile matter, your Erie Office is a disgrace to the people in northwestern Pennsylvania. Until its selective abuse of power is eliminated and ceases to be available, it will continue to be. Thank you for your time and I look forward to meeting with you in the near future.

Sincerely,

Dominick D. DiPaolo

CC: United States Attorney General Eric Holder
      United States Senator Robert Casey
      Honorable Senator Patrick Leahy, Chairman Judiciary Committee

Enclosures

CHAPTER 28

IN THE BEGINNING: CORRUPTION, MALFEASANCE, INCOMPETENCE; A DIRTY DA

It all began on a Saturday, just as another delightful Erie summer was drawing to an end on September 18, 1999 – the last September of not only the century, but the millennium.

Doug Hagmann, a private investigator and undercover Detective hired by Erie's cable television company – Cablevision – was probing an Erie bar for the alleged unauthorized use of satellite communications. Hagmann, a well-respected investigator known for his honesty and thoroughness, was probing the allegation at Cavatelli's Café at 1603 Cherry Street, was unlawfully charging admission for a Pay-For-View television event, namely a professional boxing match that was being broadcast via closed circuit TV. Reportedly, there had been many complaints to the Cablevision alleging cable theft at this location.

On the night in question, Oscar De La Hoya and Felix Trinidad, were fighting for the world title, the welter-weight WBC-IBF Championship.

Promoted by TVKO-Don King Productions, at the bar that night, and allegedly on past occasions, charged customers an admission fee to enter the establishment and watch the prize fight via an illegal cable TV hook-up. If true, it represented a federal violation of 47 USC – 605, and also possibly violations of state laws under Title 18.

Cable television piracy and theft, popular as it was in the 1990s, was nonetheless against both state and federal statutes, amounting to over $3 million annually in thefts.

Hagmann had been hired by Erie Cablevision after numerous complaints about Cavatellii charging for prize fights to determine who was stealing the cable signal, and who exactly was profiting by charging admission to illegally view the said stolen programming.

As soon as Hagmann walked into the Erie bar, the Detective was confronted by several familiar faces: A man at the door charging $2 for admission to the bar was recognized as David Cimino, a Pennsylvania State Constable. Behind the bar, taking orders and serving drinks while three television sets were broadcasting the prize fight was then District Judge John Vendetti. It was estimated that 50 to 60 patrons were jammed into this small bar.

Cimino and Laurie Oaks had formed a corporation in 1995 with Cimino as president and Oaks as secretary, and together they purchased the bar in Erie's Third Ward at 16th and Cherry Streets. Their silent partner was District Judge Vendetti, who reputedly was in a relationship with Oaks, as the two lived together in Harborcreek Township, some 12 miles east of the Third Ward. This was confirmed by Vendetti's East County YMCA membership, which listed his Harborcreek address in his "Y" membership. Obviously, Vendetti was in violation of the state law which mandates that elected District Judges must reside within the area of their jurisdiction. It is also not permitted for a judge to have a state liquor license. Legal or not, Vendetti, DiPaolo believed, usually did what he wanted. In March 1996, on the way home to Harborcreek Township from his Erie bar, he was stopped by Lawrence Park Township police and arrested for driving while intoxicated.

This corporation called Cimoaken, using letters from parts of the trio's last names, was bank-rolled by Emory Chase, an old-time bail-bondsman who, on paper, put up around $30,000 to help start the business. Oaks basically ran their business since Vendetti was a District Judge and Cimino was a State Constable, who, in 1999 made over $100,000, which is a story of its own. DiPaolo's own investigations revealed that Cimino's properties seemed to appear on the Erie County delinquent tax lists – and still were some 20 years later! "Can anyone imagine someone making that kind of money in those days who doesn't pay his taxes on a house in which he actually has rentals in the same building?" DiPaolo asked.

In addition to the illegal Pay-Per-View signal being stolen via the unauthorized hook-up, Hagmann and his men personally observed bar customers at tables doing lines of cocaine – all occurring in front of and full view of Vendetti and Cimino.

Following Hagmann's thorough investigation, including eyewitnesses accounts of crimes in progress, the private investigator submitted a full and detailed report to Erie County District Attorney Brad Foulk.

Hagmann expected action. He expected charges to be filed. He waited. And waited. But heard nothing from the DA's office. Nothing but silence.

Hagmann then began making repeated phone calls to the Erie County District Attorney's Office, but none were returned. Even the Erie Cablevision CEO made calls, but with no returns.

In frustration, Hagmann contacted the F.B.I. Erie office, at that time under the direction of Agent In Charge F.B.I. Bob Rudge. Hagmann went as far as to turn over six pages of investigative reports to Rudge and the Feds, along with a signed affidavit.

According to Hagmann, Rudge told him, "Go to Brad (Foulk). It's his game."

But when Hagmann told the Federal Agent that he had already given the detailed information to the District Attorney, the reply from Rudge was a shrug and, "I can't do anything."

What DiPaolo would later find unbelievable was that during the period that Hagmann waited for an answer from law enforcement authorities, Vendetti was actually handling cases involving the theft of cable television services. Vendetti officially ruled against those who were accused of stealing local cable television signals.

Hagmann phoned DiPaolo with an invite to lunch. He told DiPaolo he needed advice with a case he was working on. Since DiPaolo, as a Detective Sergeant, had previous worked several cases with Hagmann, and since the former cop had a great deal of respect for this investigator and his knowledge of the law, he agreed to meet him for lunch.

During their lunch, Hagmann told DiPaolo he learned that Erie Police Officer Charles Bowers, Jr., a friend of Vendetti's, got involved in Hagmann's case at the request of Foulk. Hagmann said the word was out that Vendetti was worried about cocaine and other drug use at his bar, and was telling all who would listen that it wasn't true. DiPaolo now wondered about a Judge worrying about drugs while apparently believing there was nothing wrong with the theft of cable television while Constable Cimino watched the front door.

Now, DiPaolo knew that Bowers and Vendetti had been seen together attending prize fights sponsored by Erie's boxing family, the Bizzarros and Mike Acri. But was Bowers at Cavatelli's the night of the pay-per-view fight? Hagmann could not be sure; there were many in the crowd. But he did recognize Vendetti and Cimino. DiPaolo would later learn that Officer Bowers set up a test for his friend, Vendetti, to determine whether he had any knowledge or participated in any wrongdoing, especially involving cocaine at the bar.

"Amazingly, Vendetti passed," DiPaolo mused. In those days, polygraph or lie-detector tests were used only as aids to police investigations. Results from such testing were not permissible to use as evidence in court in Pennsylvania. DiPaolo referred to them as Ouija boards. But in the late 1990s, Erie Police Officer Ken Marchant learned of a new test procedure called Computer Voice Stress Analyzer. Bowers asked Marchant to administer the so-called CVSA to Vendetti and word was that Vendetti passed, at least that's what Hagmann and others were told. Now, when Bowers became Chief of Police several years later, Marchant convinced him that using the CVSA instead of the polygraph, which is still done to this day. Like the polygraph, the CVSA is not admissible in court, but used as an investigative tool.

DiPaolo, meanwhile, told Hagmann it would be best for him to reach out to DA Foulk and request an independent test, either the CVSA or polygraph, for Vendetti. When Hagmann took DiPaolo's advice, Foulk refused and declined to prosecute. When Hagmann asked for an explanation, Foulk hung up on him.

CHAPTER 29

P. I. HAGMANN TAKES ANOTHER CHANCE

And now Hagmann told DiPaolo that he took a chance and approached Police Chief Paul DeDionisio to learn if the Chief could help him with the Cablevision investigation.

But DeDionisio, according to Hagmann, told him he knew nothing about the investigation and that Hagmann would have to approach Foulk. The Chief told Hagmann that he heard some talk about the investigation, but did not have any details. "The Chief not knowing what was going on?" DiPaolo later thought. "Imagine that!"

"But aren't Bowers and Marchant part of your police department?" Hagmann wondered, and what about Bowers... what side of the law is he on?

Bowers himself was the focus of a death investigation on July 16, 1991 at which time Bowers arrested and struggled with this young black male and the defendant died on the scene. There were conflicting statements by Bowers and other Offices who witnessed this incident, and Cunningham and Foulk assembled a Coroner's Inquest, which is like a Grand Jury that the Prosecution runs. The brought in another Attorney to handle it.

A Pittsburgh Pathologist gave testimony that would support the other Officers statements but the case was ruled an accident.

The man's family filed a Civil Rights Violation against Bowers and the City of Erie, and the City settled the case out of Court for over $400,000.00.

But DiPaolo explained to Hagmann, "This is why DeDionisio lasted so long as Chief, first with Lou Tullio as Mayor and then he did not miss a beat with Mayor Joyce Savocchio. He never got involved in controversy, never made waves, and did exactly what the mayors told him to do."

Then DiPaolo opined, "At one point in his career he was upset with the Fraternal Order of Police, the union and bargaining unit for the department, as the chief was getting beaten repeatedly by the F.O.P. in grievance matters filed by the rank and file members against him. At one point he tried to circumvent the police contract with the city, but it backfired on him and the F.O.P. considered throwing him out of the union, but stopped just short of taking a vote when he calmed down with the troops."

What's interesting about Erie, and perhaps other similar cities, is that the top ranking police officers still maintain their union membership. In most private business and industry, when union members are promoted to management positions, they are required to resign from the union as serving both represents a conflict of interest.

Such employees, however, are often protected in that should they lose their management positions they are permitted to "bump" back into non-management positions. Today, all that changed as Captains and above are removed from the Fraternal Order of Police.

DiPaolo had known DeDionisio since they were kids in grade school, graduated together and even became police officers on the same day. DiPaolo said DeDionisio began to climb the E.P.D. chain-of-command ladder in the footsteps of his father, uncle and brother.

"The problem with him is that once he got a little power, he forgot where he came from. It's like King Louie created a monster."

Even to this day, DiPaolo said, DeDionisio still has an F.O.P. license plate issued by the state on his private car. Proud of the F.O.P.? Some retired officers keep their F.O.P. plates and other identifying F.O.P. designations should the occasion arise that they are pulled over by law enforcement.

Never hurts to let a fellow bluecoat or trooper know you were a cop and expect "professional courtesies." "This is not to say it's illegal or wrong, but for DeDionisio it was hypocritical," DiPaolo thought.

DeDionisio's boss was Art Berardi, a retired Pennsylvania State Police Trooper who actually was thrown out of his own union. Berardi was hired by Mayor Tullio to straighten out the mess within the Erie Bureau of Police that Tullio knew he himself created with police appointments.

Berardi, however, was not to fulfill Tullio's desires, either.

Mario Bagnoni, a retired Erie cop who advanced to Deputy Chief and who served for more than 30 years as an outspoken City Councilman – usually speaking out against his nemesis Lou Tullio – helped remove Berardi from his city position.

"What do you expect? Berardi is cut from the same cloth as Tullio," Bagnoni said. "That's the kind of guy he would hire – someone involved in a cheating scandal while a State Trooper. And what would you expect from 'Ten percent Lou?' The guy wouldn't do anything for anyone for less than ten percent?"

DiPaolo often wondered how Tullio, after years of being paid just $28,000 in mayoral salary, and $42,000 during his last term, left any estate worth $1.6 million.

"Perhaps Bags was wrong about the ten percent," DiPaolo mused. "Could it have been more?"

DiPaolo, tongue in cheek, was known to speculate that Berardi and DeDionisio were issued rosin bags to keep their puppet strings sharp and intact for Tullio to pull. "The puppet master," DiPaolo often said.

Meanwhile, Hagmann's repeated requests were never answered, either by DA Foulk or F.B.I. Rudge or DeDionisio, three officials whom DiPaolo now knew were fast pals. Throw in Marshall Piccinni who was now the Assistant U.S. Attorney who would never go against his old boss, Foulk.

It seems that early in DeDionisio's career, he was sent to the F.B.I. Academy for training, just as many state and municipal police officers were. DiPaolo believed the policy actually allowed the Feds to have a network of "snitches" in the local departments as federal officers often had a difficult time figuring out what was happening in their communities. According to DiPaolo, whatever Rudge or the F.B.I. would request, DeDionisio was there to do it. This is why, DiPaolo reasoned, the Chief wouldn't step on Foulk's, Rudge's or Piccinni's toes in the Hagmann investigation.

But finally, he had some answers!

Hagmann learned that on September 16, 1999, just two days before his undercover probe at Cavatelli's, David Cimino of 717 West 18th Street, made a $100 contribution to DA Brad Foulk's election campaign. Then 28 days later, Angeline Vendetti, John Vendetti's mother, of 2722 Melrose Avenue in Erie, made a $300 contribution to the Foulk campaign.

As a District Judge, Vendetti himself, under the Pennsylvania Rules of Judicial Conduct, is forbidden from contributing to any political campaign. Instead, it was now clear to DiPaolo that Vendetti had used others to circumvent the rule, while enabling him to funnel money to the Brad Foulk campaign in that way.

Vendetti's office was situated in what DiPaolo considered a dump of a building at 718 West 18th Street that Vendetti himself owned. But he was told in no uncertain terms by President Judge Jess Jiuliante to move to another location because state law did not permit District Judges to own the facilities on which the county paid rent on. At one time, such an ownership/rental arrangement was allowable, but was changed by former Erie County Executive Judy Lynch.

What did Vendetti do in response? He had the deed to the building placed in his mother's name in 1994. He never moved his office to another location. Over the time he was in this elected office, the County of Erie paid thousands of dollars in rent money to the so-called owner, his mother, and when he left office in 2006, the office was rented and occupied by the new District Justice Tom Carney, Vendetti's good buddy for another six years. Even if the County was paying $1,200.00 per month (low estimate), in 18 years they would have paid over $250,000.00. DiPaolo suggested the whole block might not be worth that.

And so, it appeared to DiPaolo that the District Attorney of Erie County was accepting political contributions from two targets of what Hagmann and DiPaolo knew were illegal activities.

But at that moment in time, all Hagmann could do is wonder why Foulk and the Fed's Rudge and Piccinni were ignoring him and not taking any official action. But now he knew!

In later years, John Vendetti would marry Laurie Oaks, his partner at the bar with David Cimino, and continue to live in Harborcreek, Pennsylvania.

The bail-bondsman Emory Chase, who bank-rolled the bank investment for them, died in 2001. The executor of Chase's estate was another District Judge, Frank Abbate, who was close friends with both Vendetti and Cimino. Chase had just under a million dollars in his estate – as a result, Abbate reportedly forgave the loans Chase had made to Oaks and Cimino, and for Cavatellii at 16th and Cherry Streets for about $28,000. The mortgage satisfaction piece signed by Abbate on December 22, 2005 was notorized by John Vendetti, simply amazing.

It all helped explain for DiPaolo an event in 1994 when the former cop was a brand new District Judge and assigned to night duty. Late on a Friday night, DiPaolo set bond at $5,000 for a man charged with a domestic offense. The following Monday morning, Bondsman Emory Chase appeared in DiPaolo's office with bond papers showing that the man DiPaolo sent to jail Friday night was released from jail after posting $500 bond with Chase. The bond had been reduced from the $5,000 set by DiPaolo in an action signed by District Judge Frank Abbate of North East, Pennsylvania.

At the time, DiPaolo had no idea how Abbate got involved with not only freeing the prisoner, but lowering the bond as well. Abbate had nothing to do with Erie or this particular case. In an attempt to better learn what was happening, DiPaolo phoned his friend and ex-cop Joe Weindorf, now a District Judge in Erie's Fourth Ward.

"They took advantage of you like they did to me," Weindorf told DiPaolo.

According to what Weindorf told DiPaolo, Abbate and Chase were close friends who worked out a system – the others called it a scam – whereas Abbate signed blank bond papers.

When a person is arrested and incarcerated and the family called upon Chase for a bond, he simply visited the county prison to get the prisoner released by posting whatever bond was set by the Magistrate. But if the family could not afford the full amount set, Chase would change it on the signed blank bond papers. The only one who could change the bond is the District Judge that set the bond, but with this scam they had going, these blank bond papers were already signed by Abbate. Apparently the other District Judges, with the exception of Weindorf and DiPaolo, never complained. Which makes a reasonable person wonder why?

According to DiPaolo, Weindorf said the same thing happened to him when he first went on the bench, but he quickly contacted Abbate and told him that if it happened again Weindorf would inform the President Judge. While it never happened again to Weindorf, who had been in office for several years prior to DiPaolo's election, he told DiPaolo, "I can't believe they're still doing it!"

As a result, DiPaolo phoned Abbate with a similar message: "If you ever do that to me again, I'll go straight to the president judge."

"He tried to bullshit me and there was nothing wrong with what they were doing," DiPaolo said. After listening to Abbate's response, DiPaolo called President Judge Jiuliante anyway with the complaint.

Soon, the next time Chase appeared in DiPaolo's office, DiPaolo had the same words for the bail-bondsman.

"Yeah," Chase said. "Frank told me."

DiPaolo never spoke to Abbate or Chase again. DiPaolo would always say, "You don't have enough eyes to watch them both."

Yet, the following Christmas season, Chase brought to DiPaolo's office a poinsettia plant and bottle of liquor. DiPaolo immediately instructed his Constable, David Madurski, to return the items to Chase. (Madurski, also known as "Mud," had been DiPaolo's high school classmate, teammate and friend. Madurski, who had been a Fifth Ward constable, replaced Cimino in DiPaolo's office.)

"He was honest, had integrity, had an excellent work ethic," DiPaolo recalled. "But only after a few years, he died way before his time."

Twenty years later, the retired Abbate was still listed as a Senior Judge, one who would fill in at judge's offices when needed. "In 2020, while filling in on Erie's eastside, and after repeating racial slurs to a young black female secretary, he was relieved of his duties, hopefully for good," DiPaolo said. "He worked in the system for over 40 years. You would think he would know how to treat people."

As for Cimino, DiPaolo said, "He is still a state constable making big money. And he was ordered to pay a civil penalty of $250 for a violation of the Pennsylvania Public Ethics Act because he failed to file a statement of financial interest to the State Ethics Commission. It never stops with these guys."

CHAPTER 30

JUDGE DiPAOLO AND D.A. FOULK CLASH

But it was the year 1999 that would stand out as a red-letter year in DiPaolo's memory.

As he was a candidate for re-election as District Judge that year, he was permitted to attend political functions in his own behalf, just as DA Foulk was in his re-election campaign.

At one such event, DiPaolo heard Foulk holding court before the crowd, comparing a national political figure, who recently had been arrested, to "a piece of shit" for abusing the political system. DiPaolo, who never pulled his punches, either as a cop, or in court, or politically, knew just how frustrated the Detective Hagmann had been with Foulk. So DiPaolo, piped up:

"You have a lot of balls to make such a comparison," DiPaolo told Foulk in front of the crowd. "Isn't what that person did exactly like what you did for taking hush money from the bad guys, like in the Cablevision investigation?" Of course, the political shit hit the fan that evening, and a very loud and boisterous argument ensued.

"You're no better than the 'piece of shit' you were complaining about," DiPaolo told Foulk, again in front of the awe-struck group.

From that day forward, the two public officials never spoke to one another again.

As for Vendetti and Cimino, no action was ever taken against them.

Although the paths of DiPaolo and Foulk would often cross, the two would continue to ignore one another.

Which was fine with DiPaolo.

But Foulk would not forget.

Another disgrace to the minor judiciary in Erie County in North East occurred, in DiPaolo's opinion, when Gerald L. Alonge, Abbate's friend, ran for District Judge when Frank Abbate also retired in 2005.

Alonge, who won the seat and took office in 2006, was the recipient of five separate complaints filed against him by five women. One was a 17-year-old who accused Alonge of stalking, harassment and telephone harassment. The four others, all adult women and attorneys recently admitted to the bar, were reportedly telephoned repeatedly at their offices and homes by Alonge. One alleged that Alonge followed her and her children on Halloween night, even when she pulled into her own driveway.

The complaints against the District Judge were eventually heard by the Pennsylvania Judicial Conduct Board, which took testimony from the women and sent the case to the next level: The Court of Judicial Discipline. That court determined and concluded that Alonge brought his Judicial Office into disrepute. The court handed him a 30-day suspension, with the resultant loss of thousands of dollars.

Alonge actually had the balls to seek re-election in 2011, but was overwhelmingly defeated by Scott Hammer, who DiPaolo has recognized as the township's "real Judge" ever since.

CHAPTER 31

THE COMMONWEALTH WEIGHS IN WITH MORE HARASSMENT

In November 2010, the Consumer Protection Division of the Pennsylvania Office of the Attorney General, sued a locally-operated company, Unicredit of America, basically a collection outfit, for alleged unethical practices.

By sheer coincidence, Unicredit's business offices were located behind the office of District Judge Dominick DiPaolo. Although there was no other connection between the two offices, DiPaolo had in the past held hearings in connection with civil complaints Unicredit filed against consumers, and judgments were filed against the defendants. The so-called unethical practices occurred after the real court-issued judgments were filed: The collection agency attempted to apply pressure on the defendants to force them to pay up. It is alleged the company threatened the defendants, including threatening to take their vehicles. Anything to collect what was owed.

From the start that November, DiPaolo could see the entire episode stunk of politics.

Pennsylvania Attorney General Tom Corbett, a Republican, was running for Governor. The polls a month earlier in October 2010 showed Corbett running behind in Erie County. What better way to make some loud noise than to take down an established business?

But it later became common knowledge that the Consumer Protection Division had a complaint against Unicredit that had been filed 18 months before, but had never taken action. Why now? The answer was obvious. "Attorney Leslie Grey didn't know what to do with it," DiPaolo said.

"Andrea Amicangelo, of Northwest Legal Services, received the complaint and turned it over to the Office of the Attorney General, but they never followed up on it. And Amicangelo never called Grey to follow up. Then Grey used it to help Corbett during the election."

Normally, according to established procedure, when the Consumer Protection Division receives a complaint, the proper first step is to notify the company in writing, advising the company that a complaint was filed while giving them the opportunity to respond with their version of the issue in question. But not in the Unicredit case! Instead, it appeared to be an opportunity for the attorney general to get headlines – which Corbett did. But he had to have a full Republican cast to pull this off. Judge Dunlavey shut down the business with one hearing, where was the due process?

Demonstrating just how unusual this action by the Attorney General was, Erie Attorney Gary Nash, who ran the Office of Consumer Protection for 12 years from 1974 to 1986, was outraged with how this investigation proceeded. Nash went to the newspaper, but was ignored. Not a word of his criticism printed. He even gave a six-page notarized affidavit that the newspaper also ignored.

Corbett named Attorney Leslie Grey, of his office, to mastermind this horror show. When they learned that the collection agency and buildings in the strip plaza were owned by Al Covatto and that his cousin was District Judge Dominick DiPaolo, the local media had a field day with corruption rumors. Or, DiPaolo thought, reporter Ed Palattella did.

DiPaolo believes that when the reporter heard DiPaolo's name in connection with Covatto, "I think the ace reporter's pants got wet – another story where he could blast me like he did in the purse party raid."

Of course, there was no evidence linking DiPaolo to the investigation other than being a relative of Covatto's. DiPaolo's offices were located in that strip plaza for over 20 years, Erie County government having selected that space two decades earlier. Over the years, Covatto and the county negotiated the rent, which was in line with other District Justice offices through the city and county. DiPaolo, however, believed there was no doubt it was the most attractive, cleanest and most handicapped accessible of all.

DiPaolo believes the reporter's crusade against him was aided by outside help, or, in DiPaolo's words, "outside lies."

DiPaolo had been having problems with the elected constable in his office, Frank Altadonna, and had long suspected some aspects of the constable's work. In December 2010, a month after the Unicredit investigation began, DiPaolo suspected Altadonna was not serving defendants with civil papers, but still putting in for payments as though the papers were served. For example, a woman who was handed a judgment against her was never served to appear at the hearing, although Altadonna claimed her served her. But she had moved from the address where Altadonna claimed she was served a year before. Immediately DiPaolo fired the constable.

According to DiPaolo, one of his office workers, Shelly Banta, Altadonna's sister, tried to help her brother, but violated office security procedures in the process. When DiPaolo learned of it, he confronted the worker, who had first denied her actions, but then admitted to what she had done. She was fired two days later. Banta filed for unemployment but the County of Erie and DiPaolo opposed it. After many hearings and all the way to the Courts of PA. It was denied.

DiPaolo believes that both these now unemployed former employees, in retribution for being fired, ran to Palattella and to the Feds.

As a result, Palattella began his war of words on DiPaolo through many newspaper articles spread out over months and even years.

"It seemed his M.O. was apparent to all," DiPaolo would later say. "This so-called investigation began in November 2010, just six months before I would be running for re-election in the May 2011 primary."

Now, from November 3, 2010 until December 29, 2010, Palattella penned 12 articles concerning this story, some of them with co-worker Lisa Thompson. DiPaolo's name appeared in seven of the 12 articles.

Then, from February to May 2011, Palattella and Thompson wrote 16 additional articles, with DiPaolo's name in 10 of them.

On May 4, 2011, Palattella wrote another Unicredit article, listing DiPaolo's name – less than two weeks before the May 17 election.

In fact, Erie County Judge Dunlavey, in a letter to Judge DiPaolo, said he did not know what courtroom Palattella was reporting from. Dunlavey also sent DiPaolo a transcript of the Unicredit hearing so that DiPaolo could see for himself that Dunlavey's comments did not match up with what the reporter had written about DiPaolo. (Many will recall the controversy involving the Judge, now a retired Army Major General specializing in intelligence, over interrogation techniques used while Dunlavey was Commandant of the Guantanamo Bay, Cuba, Detention Camps.)

"It was without a doubt the reporter's and Erie Times-News' hatchet job on me," DiPaolo said.

As soon as DiPaolo received the transcript from Dunlavey, he phoned the Times-News and arranged for a meeting with Executive Editor Rick Sayers. When DiPaolo arrived at the paper, he was greeted by Sayers and Pat Howard, then managing editor of news. DiPaolo brought clips of the paper, articles by Palattella quoting Dunlavey as saying DiPaolo created a ghost system of justice, that DiPaolo's office should be looked into and that the Judicial Conduct Board should be called to determine if DiPaolo will be investigated. DiPaolo tossed the actual transcript, however, on Sayers' desk and demanded, "Show me where Dunlavey said these things." While Sayers was saying he'd take up the matter with Palattella, Howard added, "Well, you are a stockholder in Unicredit." Typical, uninformed reporter, shooting from the hip without the facts, DiPaolo thought. DiPaolo left, saying, "You'll hear from my lawyers."

Palattella had also written in his articles that F.B.I. Special Agent Gerald Clark and Assistant U.S. Attorney Marshall Piccinni attended the hearing, sitting quietly in the courtroom, but declined comment when they left. DiPaolo knows they were the reporter's snitches. "Do these names sound familiar?" DiPaolo thought to himself. "Think of the purse party scam in 2007."

"He was trying to make his readers think that I must have really fucked up since the feds were there," DiPaolo later said. "But these two probably get lost on their way to work!"

Sayers phoned DiPaolo the next day, saying he spoke with Palattella that he might have made a mistake. "Fine, I want a retraction," DiPaolo responded. Sayers indicated he would speak to the others about it, but the retraction never came and DiPaolo filed his lawsuit against the reporter and the paper.

As for Howard's comments about DiPaolo being a stockholder, DiPaolo said that was not true, either. "That's the problem with Erie being a one-newspaper town. They say and write what they want and no one can write a different account."

But there was more! During 2012, Palattella wrote 21 articles, nine in 2013, seven in 2014 and one in 2015. Thirty-eight in all, and DiPaolo's name appeared only once. So it appeared to DiPaolo that the reporter was making a career out of this investigation. His pal Marjorie Diehl of the Pizza Bomber Case had been convicted, so it seemed to DiPaolo that the reporter could not write in the newspaper about her and her crooked friends, settling instead on a book with his F.B.I. friend, Jerry Clark.

Why was DiPaolo's name then in only one article? The election was over and he had won. The answer was clear.

In the Unicredit case, the "target" was Michael Covatto, Al Covatto's son, who was the person who actually ran Unicredit in addition to Attorney Larry D'Ambrosio. So the Feds, Jerry Clark and Marshall Piccinni, in an attempt to tie DiPaolo to the case, offered Michael Covatto immunity. But he had only a day to decide.

"It's called Queen for a Day," DiPaolo said. "Can you imagine the balls of these Feds? But it really didn't surprise me as they both fucked up the Pizza Bomber case." (To be discussed later in the following pages.)

But Covatto advised the Feds he did not need immunity as he did not commit a crime or do anything wrong. He further told them that Judge DiPaolo had nothing at all to do with Unicredit, and that, as usual, the Feds were again being fooled by those lying to them, especially DiPaolo's fired former employees. His attorney, Michael Gramal, told the Feds his client was willing to take a polygraph, truth serum, anything the Feds offered to show that both DiPaolo and Covatto had nothing to do with the case. Of course, no tests were administered. By the time it was over, from 2010 to 2015, reporter Palattella had written 92 articles on Unicredit. No one went to jail. No one paid a fine – even though there was a judicial order from Michael Dunlavey that over $600,000 be paid in civil penalties, but that was rescinded.

On January 7, 2015, Attorney Grey, on behalf of the Office of the Attorney General, filed a motion of "No Judgment" against Unicredit and Michael Covatto. The investigation was over. To DiPaolo, it had been nothing more than a fucking waste of time and money.

Strange, DiPaolo thought, that Palattella missed this conclusion and neither he nor anyone at the newspaper wrote an article informing the public. No 93rd article. Very strange, indeed! Also, DiPaolo later learned that the Feds closed their investigation as well. After filing a Right-To-Know Act request, helped by Attorney John Carlson, DiPaolo found that the Feds had accumulated 1,724 pages of reports in the investigation and grand jury proceedings. And nothing came of it. It did not surprise DiPaolo.

"The OAG had over 3,000 pages of bullshit investigation reports. I always believed they would have a hard time finding an elephant in a phone booth," he later said. "They just proved it."

By March of 2012, cases against Unicredit were making their way through the Erie County Court system. In one, Erie County Judge Michael Dunlavey presided over a hearing to decide a motion filed by Attorney Michael Kruszewski, representing Mark and Christine Lashinger, to dismiss the judgment that had been filed against them by Judge DiPaolo for non-payment of a $845 medical bill. Unicredit had earlier appeared in DiPaolo's court, presented evidence that Christine Lashinger failed to pay Unicredit the $50 a month she had allegedly agreed to pay. As a result, Unicredit had filed a civil suit, and DiPaolo granted a judgment in the company's favor. Pretty cut and dried stuff as far as Civil Court business goes in the Magisterial Court System.

But in his motion to dismiss, Kruszewski, the Lashinger's attorney, claimed neither the Lashinger's nor the OB/GYN medical firm that treated Mrs. Lashinger, have offices in Erie's Sixth Ward and therefore Judge DiPaolo had no jurisdiction over the case or authority to award a judgment. Yet the facts of this matter clearly showed that the medical firm was indeed located within the Sixth Ward on West 23rd Street in 2009 when Lashinger received services and failed to pay the $845 she owed. Also, it is common textbook forbearance law that when a creditor and debtor enter into a signed agreement, just as Unicredit and Lashinger had, and when the $50 monthly payment was not made, then the agreement was in default. Again, pretty simple stuff in the world of contract law. She was paying Unicredit, not the OB/GYN.

But the next day, the Erie Times-News headline, "Judge Tosses $845 Medical Bill" over an article by Reporter Kevin Flowers, a co-worker and minion of Palattella's, appeared out of place. Judge Dunlavey said that since Unicredit did not show up for the hearing, he was compelled to strike the judgment. DiPaolo believes Dunlavey must have forgotten that he previously ordered Unicredit closed and shut down, and with no hearing. The notice of the Lashinger's hearing before Dunlavey was sent to a vacant address. No one knew of the hearing until it appeared in the newspaper the next day. What a system! DiPaolo thought.

What's more, DiPaolo knew that most good journalists would have checked out the information to determine if the medical firm was indeed in the Sixth Ward rather than depending upon the inaccuracies and lies in an attorney's motion. But it now seemed that the newspaper was clearly interested in blasting DiPaolo, the facts be damned. And the Lashingers showed everyone that they did not pay their bill after receiving treatment. Just two more deadbeats, DiPaolo thought. A woman gets professional services from a doctor and then blows him off for payment.

CHAPTER 32

A THICK SKIN, YES;
BUT ENOUGH IS ENOUGH!

Cops and Judges know that if they are to survive in their chosen professions for long, they must adapt to the criticism that comes with the territory and grow thick skins. DiPaolo had been a cop and now he was a Judge, so the task became doubly difficult. DiPaolo, however, was up to it. Normally he did not let the day to day criticism, usually by those whom were the targets of his criminal investigations or on the losing ends of his judicial rulings, upset him nor did he linger long over the criticism.

But now he had enough of the harassment, misrepresentations and outright lying. Marshall Piccinni, the U.S. Attorney's Office, the F.B.I.'s Jerry Clark, Leslie Grey, and the Office of the Attorney General and Ed Palattella of the Erie Times and his minions now appeared to be telling anyone willing to listen that Judge DiPaolo's actions were questionable. Furthermore, Erie County Judge Ernie DiSantis, who had been a professional and personal friend with DiPaolo for many years, abandoned the District Judge in great haste.

That was never more clear to DiPaolo than on a sultry morning in July 2013 while DiPaolo was taking his turn presiding over early procedures in criminal cases in Central Court. Court was held in Erie County Council Chambers on the first floor of the Erie County Courthouse.

The room itself is larger than the courtrooms of the individual District Judges adjoining their offices, but not quite as large as most of the Common Pleas Judges' Courtrooms. The problem with holding Central Court in council chambers, however, stems from the lack of appropriate facilities for such a purpose. For example, the corridors leading to Central Court are often congested, choked with those waiting to appear in court: victims, witnesses, police, defendants.

"There was nothing District Judges could do to alleviate the crowding," DiPaolo would explain, since all those needed for criminal court procedures were subpoenaed by police and were required to be there. Each case had a number of these people waiting for their hearings."

On this steamy morning, however, the public defender assigned to DiPaolo's court was attending sentencing in a courtroom on the second floor before a Common Pleas Judge and late in arriving for Central Court. Making matters worse was that the two-week term of Erie County Criminal Court was underway and most the public defender's staff were busy in other court cases.

In DiPaolo's court, District Attorney Jack Daneri was handing the prosecutorial side of the cases, the first four scheduled involving the Public Defender's Office. But the cases scheduled for 9:00, 9:15, 9:30 and 10 a.m. could not be conducted as the public defender was not present to represent clients. The log jam in the courtroom exacerbated the situation in the hallways with dozens of people jammed into the area. Eventually, DiPaolo, waiting in Central Court, and Daneri, who had gone back to the DA's office, were notified that the public defender had arrived. DiPaolo returned to the bench and Daneri was ready to go, as was the Public Defender. Suddenly, DiPaolo recalled, "the door swung open and President Judge DiSantis and Tom Aaron approached the bench." It was rare for a Common Pleas judge to appear in Central Court, especially the President Judge.

"Hello, Your Honor," DiPaolo greeted his longtime friend. "What's up?" What do I owe this honor?

But DiSantis was apparently in no mood for pleasantries and he began shouting, loud enough for all in the courtroom to hear.

"I'll tell you what the fuck is up! I'm tired of County Council bitching about all these fucking people in the hallway!"

DiPaolo was taken aback. He did not understand why his longtime friend was addressing him in that tone or manner. Sarcastically, he turned in his chair and looked behind him as though searching for another person the Judge might be addressing. "You talking to me?" he asked.

"I'm getting fucking tired of getting calls from Councilman Leone!" DiPaolo recalled DiSantis saying.

DiPaolo explained the delay caused by the absence of the Public Defender. He told of having his own secretary phone the Public Defender's Office, and of being informed that all the attorneys were in court and they had no one to cover. DiPaolo told DiSantis that the public defender assigned to Central Court, Kevin Kallenbach, had arrived only minutes earlier.

But DiSantis continued, "If I have to come down here again, I'll start scheduling your cases, one every hour, so there won't be that many people at one time in the hall and you'll be here until 7 at night." DiPaolo recalled that Court Administrator Aaron, all the while, was smiling.

DiSantis apparently knew full well that DiPaolo was more than pissed at this unnecessary scolding because DiPaolo just stared at DiSantis without saying a word.

But then, as fast as the President Judge erupted, he quickly calmed down. "Dominick, I am just pissed at Council. They break my balls all the time over this shit."

Then DiSantis asked, "How's Pat?" He was referring to DiPaolo's son, Patrick, the Principal at East High School who was extremely ill at the time and passed away a month later.

DiSantis quickly left the courtroom, with Aaron trying to keep pace about a step behind him. DiPaolo said Aaron was known around the courthouse as "King Ernie's lap dog" and he seemed to enjoy "his master yelling" at DiPaolo.

During the outburst, District Attorney Daneri had entered the courtroom and when DiSantis left, he asked to approach the bench. "He had the courtesy to ask to approach, not like King Ernie, who just walked right up like gang busters," DiPaolo said. "It's a courtesy that all professionals give to Judges."

"What was that all about with Ernie?" Daneri asked.

"He's the one who wanted to be President Judge, but he can't handle the pressure," DiPaolo replied.

But pressure or not, DiPaolo knew the behavior was not only unprofessional, but the language inappropriate at best for any officer of the court, especially a President Judge.

The threat to punish DiPaolo by making him stay late also seemed appalling to the District Judge. The close personal relationship that DiPaolo and DiSantis had shared for many years ended that day.

"Had the shoe been on the other foot, I would have never addressed a friend in that fashion no matter how upset I might have been," DiPaolo later said. "When we talk about people who forgot where they came from, that became a perfect example."

What's more, Attorney John Melarango, the assigned Bankruptcy Court trustee for the Covattos, appeared to DiPaolo to be lying about the District Judge and his family, on one occasion telling U.S. District Court Judge Sean McLaughlin and federal employees mistruths about the DiPaolos' involvement with Unicredit, statements which McLaughlin relayed to other federal employees who were DiPaolo's friends.

Meanwhile, Reporter Palattella, in a front page article in the April 17, 2011 Sunday newspaper, actually published a Mafia-like family tree of DiPaolo's family tree. The "tree" listed DiPaolo's deceased father and Al Covatto's deceased mother in an attempt to show the relationship between a brother and sister and two cousins. Interesting that no one had ever denied the relationship. To DiPaolo's thinking, it was just another over-the-top example of Yellow Journalism, and only 30 days before DiPaolo's re-election bid. And it put DiPaolo over the top as now his father and aunt were dragged into the story. Thick-skinned, yes. But when Dominick DiPaolo's family is attacked in such a personal way, it became the proverbial straw that broke the camel's back. Now it was personal.

DiPaolo easily won the May primary against John Little, coming out on top of both Democratic and Republican ballots and was assured to win the November general election.

Even with the lies of Denise Altadonna, sister of Frank and Shelly Altadonna, who was working as a campaign volunteer at the polls for John Little, she was telling the voters DiPaolo was corrupt with the Unicredit case and his wife and daughter corrupt with the purse party and were going to be indicted. This confirmed to DiPaolo that the two fired Altadonna's were giving bullshit info to the Feds and Fast Eddie.

But Anne Grunewald, the Sixth Ward Republican Party Chairwoman, a friend of DiPaolo's for many years, phoned him in August 2011 with interesting news: She had been contacted by Debbie Gallagher, who worked for Republican State Representative Curt Sonney and who wanted Grunewald to help organize a write-in campaign against DiPaolo.

"Are you nuts?" Grunewald asked Gallagher. "How are you going to beat Dom DiPaolo? Grunewald told DiPaolo the woman responded, "I'm not, but maybe I can get the appointment from Governor Corbett when DiPaolo gets indicted."

"Indicted?" Grunewald said. "Where did you get that from?" To that, the woman said, "Don't you read Ed Palattella's stories in the Times-News?" But Grunewald told her, "Don't believe everything you read in that newspaper!" When Grunewald told Gallagher that she should run in May if she really wanted to, Gallagher reportedly told her she was going to run in May, but when she didn't, Sonney advised her to register as an Independent, which she did. She told Grunewald that Sonney said that if DiPaolo went down, Sonney would get her the appointment from the governor. When Gallagher mentioned that the articles in the paper about DiPaolo and kickbacks did not look good, Grunewald again advised her not to believe everything in that newspaper.

The newspaper jumped on the story of Gallagher's announcement to oppose DiPaolo. This time, the lengthy November 2 article headlined "DiPaolo Challenged," was written by reporter Lisa Thompson, another of Palattella's minions.. But despite the publicity, Gallagher did not fare well on election day, garnering a mere 417 votes to DiPaolo's 2512. As for Grunewald's advice on not believing everything Gallagher read, that was correct as well. DiPaolo was not indicted. The entire investigation was a scam.

CHAPTER 33

THE JUDGE GOES TO COURT

Following the 2011 General Election, during which Judge Dominick DiPaolo won his fourth six-year term of office, DiPaolo knew the time had come to avail himself and his family of the legal system he had spent a career and a lifetime defending.

DiPaolo believed in that legal system, even after those rare occasions when he was at odds with the system. He had dedicated his adult life to working within the system, never ever attempting to go around or bypass the law.

And so it was that immediately following that successful 2011 election, DiPaolo filed a lawsuit against the Times Publishing Company, goerie. com, reporters Edward Palattella, Jr., Lisa Thompson, and Michael Maciag, alleging incorrect reporting, defamation of character, and libel.

DiPaolo knew that in courts of law, not in newspaper articles, especially those appearing to him to be akin to tabloid reporting, each side of the issue is heard. Never rumors. Never innuendos. Never smear campaigns. Never attempt political assassinations just weeks or days before an election. What's heard in real-life courts of law is real and sworn testimony. Real and corroborated evidence. Real exhibits. Real testimony. Only in that way, when both sides are heard under oath and penalty of perjury, can fair and accurate judgments be made.

DiPaolo's son Patrick, who was very ill and bedridden, was very upset with the newspaper articles and told his father, "I hope you're not going to let these people get away with this."

"Absolutely not, I promise you!" DiPaolo responded. So the suit was filed.

And the case dragged on for six long years. There were many depositions. From them, DiPaolo knew that Palattella had misled the court about their relationship.

But despite that, Erie County Judge John Bozza's rulings favored DiPaolo. Even when the newspaper appealed every ruling, many appeals as far as the Pennsylvania Supreme Court, DiPaolo's side still prevailed. He know it would. He knew he was right and the paper, or, those who worked for it, were wrong.

As DiPaolo saw it:

- The Unicredit case that began in 2010, with Reporter Palattella writing scores of articles about it, never saw the light of day in a real life courtroom.

- No charges were ever brought against the Covattos.

- No charges were ever brought against Judge DiPaolo.

- Many thousands of dollars were spent by the Office of the Attorney General, the F.B.I. and the Erie Times-News.

And all for what?

To embarrass a popular judge and his family, and allegedly help a politician whom DiPaolo believed gave new meaning to the term "low life."

As DiPaolo saw and lived it, it was all a well-documented conspiracy against him.

"And as usual, the bad guys fucked up at the end," a prominent longtime court observer was overheard saying. Palattella took a shot at him in 2002 suggesting DiPaolo used his stamp machine illegally, then in 2007 with the purse party and now in 2010 with Unicredit. Nothing worked.

As stated, it seemed that the only article Palattella did not write about Unicredit was in January 2015 when Leslie Grey, representing the Office of the Attorney General, filed a motion to finally bring to an end the Unicredit case that had been brought against Michael Covatto.

No criminal charges. No civil charges. "And the federalis – Piccinni and his boy, Clark, both now left holding their dicks again, instead of purses," DiPaolo later said. This is exactly what happens when politicians attempt to control the criminal justice system, DiPaolo thought.

In both investigations, neither the F.B.I. or OAG ever asked DiPaolo to give a statement; he was not even talked to!

What kind of phony bullshit was that? DiPaolo often thought.

In July of 2017, DiPaolo was advised by his lawyers, Pete and Matt Kurzwicz of Pittsburgh, that they were in agreement with the Times Publishing Company's attorneys that the next step in the case was a jury trial. But both sides were willing to try mediation in front of an out-of-town attorney who would be like a referee. Although DiPaolo did not have to agree to mediation, he was advised that the outcome need not be mandatory and that a jury trial would always be an option and the mediation would not be held against him. DiPaolo thought what did he have to loose.

So, after six hours of mediation and negotiations, DiPaolo ultimately agreed to settle the case. Under a signed non-disclosure agreement, neither side could publicly talk about the amount of the settlement. DiPaolo had no problem with the non-disclosure. He told his lawyers that he believes money was not always a reward, but a victory in itself is priceless. "Naturally, the newspaper did not admit to any wrongdoing."

Fortunately for the average, common citizens, those politicians rarely win.

As for Palattella, DiPaolo now believed that instead of reporting the news, Palattella simply wanted to make the news.

Unfortunately, by 2017 Judge DiPaolo and his wife Janet lost their son, Patrick. But as soon as DiPaolo got back to Erie after receiving the settlement, his first stop was at Calvary Cemetery, where he told Pat what had transpired, and that the case was over.

On August 2, 2019, slightly over a year since DiPaolo settled his defamation law-suit against Palattella and the Erie Times-News, the Erie School District dedicated a school and named it to honor Patrick J. DiPaolo.

The Patrick J. DiPaolo Student Success Center at Emerson-Gridley School, which houses the district's alternative education program, was dedicated to the former school district principal and coach who had been the first principal of the Flagship Transition School for trouble youth in 2004.

"Pat had done a tremendous job of laying the groundwork for this very important aspect of education," DiPaolo said. "This was now the second honor accorded to Pat as the auditorium at then Central High, where he coached football and was assistant principal, his first administrative position, was named the Patrick J. DiPaolo Memorial Auditorium."

At the dedication and reception for the auditorium, the Superintendent of Schools, Dr. Jay Badams, and School Board President Ed Brzezinski were upset that despite a news release being sent to all the news media, only the television stations but not the newspaper, covered the event. The same happened when the school was dedicated by Superintendent Brian Polito and School Board President Frank Petrunger Jr. Nothing carried in the Erie Times-News, Erie's only daily print media.

This was the first time in many years that the district named a school after one of its own.

"It is therefore no surprise that Ed Palattella was the reporter assigned to the Erie School District beat, covering all the school news," DiPaolo said. "He simply showed his ignorance, bias and hatefulness by not covering either event as not one word about them appeared in his rag of a newspaper. This low-life refused to honor someone who gave so much to kids and the community. Some 12,000 students and 1,500 teachers and employees honored him not once, but twice."

Pat's lifelong dedication to education and sports during his years of teaching and coaching made a positive difference in the lives of countless student/athletes. Often at his own expense, Pat provided food, clothing, money and athletic equipment, as well as moral support and mentoring to students in need. His keen understanding of the importance of post-secondary education led him to assist many students in attaining college and university scholarships. If not for Pat DiPaolo, many of these students could not have enrolled in college on their own.

After Pat passed away, a memorial scholarship was founded in his honor and in only seven years, 78 scholarships worth more than $78,000 were awarded to Erie County student/athletes. His lifelong work and legacy continues to be memorialized in this meaningful way. "Palattella's bias toward me in his coverage of the purse party scam and the Unicredit fiasco, 92 articles in all, was finally held accountable for his yellow journalism. It all caught up to him when we filed the law suit against him and the newspaper," DiPaolo said.

But DiPaolo said that to get back at him, "what does he do but target our son, who died at 44, and who did more for the Erie community than Palattella could ever do. To think he could be so low in his life to do something like that – what did Pat DiPaolo do to Palattella? Just no integrity at all. He proved not only in these incidents, but in many stories that he doesn't report the news without bias and without his own opinions, which should be crucial in accuracy and content and perspective. But he misses the facts regularly."

According to DiPaolo, up through 2021, the Patrick J. DiPaolo Student Success Center rarely appears in an articles about the Erie School District.

"It's sad that many Erie residents have no idea there is such a school with that name," DiPaolo said. "They should have been informed by their newspaper on August 3, 2019, the day after it was named, but never did."

CHAPTER 34

THE PIZZA BOMBER INVESTIGATION
ANOTHER F.B.I. FIASCO

In August 2003, a suburb just outside Erie, Pennsylvania, made national headlines. It was the scene of what later became known as the "Pizza Bomber Case".

A collection of local misfits, all of them characterized as degenerates, dysfunctional and mentally-challenged, somehow convinced – perhaps brainwashed – a pizza delivery driver to wear a collar bomb around his neck in what would become a foiled bank robbery. When the horrified driver realized the bomb was not a dummy, but a live explosive, he pleaded with police to help him. But before the police bomb squad could intervene, the collar bomb was detonated, immediately ending the life of the helpless and luckless pizza man.

Whether the victim was actually a part of the bank robbery conspiracy still remains a point for discussion. However, F.B.I. Agent Clark appeared to have made a career of just that one case. For seven years, culminating in 2010, Clark and the Feds worked the case, which did not involve either master criminals or rocket scientists.

Why this investigation, involving the incredulous granting of immunity to the crime's planner, took seven years is still up for debate. But murder probes are not the F.B.I.'s forte. In all reality, the F.B.I. is entirely unfamiliar with homicide investigations. This might have been Clark's one and only murder investigation.

DiPaolo often wondered why Clark, who had at one time been the Acting Agent in Charge of Erie's F.B.I. office, had not joined the others during the raid at DiPaolo's home. Was it because Clark had worked cases with the former Erie Detective Sergeant and did not want to embarrass him?

Only later would DiPaolo learn that the probable and actual reason Clark did not participate in the purse raid was because his wife, Danielle, had hosted a similar purse party at Clark's Erie County home. DiPaolo would forever wonder: Why was it okay for an F.B.I. Agent's wife to host such a party, but not okay for Judge DiPaolo's wife to do so?

Eventually, DiPaolo would conclude that such arbitrary rules applied to only a certain few, while the F.B.I. was good at granting even itself immunity. "It's like Donald Trump, the worst U.S. President in history with his corrupt friends convicted of felonies and Trump pardoning them so they wouldn't shit the bed on him," DiPaolo said.

Again, credibility and even morality became the heart of the matter in DiPaolo's mind.

Only in Erie can a federal law enforcement officer give a murderer immunity and then be handed a judgeship. To DiPaolo, it appeared the Piccinni granted immunity to Floyd Stockton, the main plotter in the Pizza Bomber Case.

Real Investigators and Prosecutors who are seasoned and know what they are doing, never give someone who is responsible for killing immunity.

It reminded DiPaolo of when he and ADA Tim Lucas went to Cleveland, Ohio, in early 1980s to interview a guy who had information on the "Ash Wednesday" Frank Bolo Dovishaw, contract killing. Robert Dorler wanted immunity from prosecution. Lucas, after some talks, granted immunity with the exception of him committing or being involved in murder or child molestation.

Stupid Dorler who thought DiPaolo and Lucas came in yesterday's mail, gave info on the hit, who was involved, and who did what and who was the shooter, and where the gun was dumped in a lake.

After months of real police work, it was proven Dorler was the trigger and he and all his boys all went to jail. Dorler got life with no parole, and the immunity deal went out the window.

This bank robbery investigation turned out to be a cluster fuck from the get go. The Pennsylvania State Police were the first called to the scene as it was their jurisdiction. When the bomb went off, the AFT (Alcohol, Tobacco & Firearms) appeared, and then the F.B.I. arrived as it was determined the bank was robbed (Federal Reserve Funds).

Now the cluster fuck started as all three agencies wanted to take the lead, but the Feds won out as the Erie County D.A. Brad Foulk sold out the Pennsylvania State Police and he let his buddy Marshall Piccinni and the Feds take the investigation. Foulk later would brag he made the call for Marshall as they never had a case of this magnitude.

It took years for the Feds to finally put something together as these nitwits had them on the ropes.

They were given the name of Floyd Stockton who was in Erie in 2003, and was on the lam and was in Washington State. The Feds flew to Washington State and Stockton, like Colonel Klink said, "I know nothing."

He gave a statement claiming he had no information. He was given a polygraph test and passed, and he was finally cleared by the F.B.I. with having no connection to the Pizza Bomber Case. Who cleared him? Piccinni and Clark.

Then years later, they received more information on Stockton.

Piccinni offered Stockton, "A Queen for a Day" (sound familar... the same he offered Michael Covatto in the scam Unicredit Case). There are two types of immunity. Use immunity which the person gets limited protection, and full immunity which means they get complete protection.

Historically when Investigators and Prosecutors know the person is involved in the crime, especially in a murder investigation, you give them use immunity, charge them as a co-conspirator. They testify at court truthfully, then the charges are reduced at sentencing, making the judge know of their cooperation. That's the break they get.

Stockton told them it was his idea to rob a bank, and use a pizza deliveryman, He helped build the collar bomb.

On the day of the bank job, he carried the collar bomb to a van, placed the collar bomb on Brian Wells neck, tightened it and locked it.

Stockton then as a participant, went to a gas station near the bank to wait for Wells who was supposed to bring him the money after the bank job. Now here is the kicker. Stockton told Wells the bomb wasn't real. Everyone knows the rest of the story.

Stockton was brought to the Grand Jury, told that story and Piccinni in his infinite wisdom granted Stockton full immunity, no co-conspirator, no murder charge, nothing. And Jerry Clark encouraged it. But Stockton had to testify in court, but just years earlier they cleared him of any involvement. Simply amazing.

Then all geared up for the camera's. U.S. Attorney Mary Beth Buchanan made the long awaited announcement of indictments in the "Pizza Bomber Case". She named all the misfits charged, but no mention of Stockton. Piccinni and Clark gleaming in the camera lights like a cat that caught a canary.

Piccinni was asked by the media who made the bomb? He hesitated and looked at Buchanan and said, "I don't know." He didn't know if he should give up Stockton at that time.

Then out of nowhere, Buchanan spurts out... "But Wells played a limited role." What evidence did anyone have that Wells played any role other than the victim?

It was like a fucking dog and pony show. Now you know why this was a cluster fuck. Thanks to Foulk sticking his nose in.

At the trial, Floyd Stockton was on the Government's witness list, but never showed up. It was later learned he was recovering from open heart surgery, 10 or 12 days before the trial started.

Floyd Stockton pulled off the deal of his life. It was his idea to do the bank job with the other nitwits, which they did. And Brian Wells was killed. Full immunity, no charges, no testimony at trial. He got away completely free, thanks to Piccinni and Clark. Totally disgraceful. Brian Wells brother went on national T.V. questioning the integrity and intelligence of Clark and Piccinni. National FOX News reporter Geraldo Rivera said, he had no idea why the Feds gave full immunity to Stockton when learning he was involved from day one. Why would you do that?

Just think Piccinni and Clark both knew this low life Stockton was on the lam from the State of Washington for rape. It was determined that the victim of this rape was a 19-year-old developmentally disabled girl, of which he was convicted.

Where did the ethical, moral, and legal obligation of Piccinni and Clark go in freeing this piece of shit of any responsibility. WOW!

Larry D'Ambrosio was the Personal Attorney for the wing-nut Marjorie Diehl for forty years who was involved in the Pizza Bomber Case. At her trial, D'Ambrosio was called by her Attorney as a witness for her. Both Piccinni and Clark had the ass for him as he fucked them over when he testified about the conversation he had with her about the bank job.

When Piccinni was cross examining D'Ambrosio, he gave his answer and referred to Piccinni as "Marshall". Piccinni was so pissed he started yelling at D'Ambrosio saying "Don't you ever call me Marshall." The Jury snickered. Real professional. He took his eye off the ball.

A few years later, they were very happy to hear D'Ambrosio's name in the Unicredit case, as it was payback time to get even. Or at least they thought. That was another fuck up on the Fed's part.

Backing all this up was a television documentary on the Pizza Bomber Case called "Evil Genius." Trey Borzillieri, of TMZ Television and who directed the documentary, publicly stated that Floyd Stockton was given immunity by Piccinni, and never charged. It was stated that Stockton got away with murder, and that justice was not served in that case. This was televised nationally.

As for the reporter's pal and co-author Clark, the former F.B.I. Agent has made statements to the effect that solving the Pizza Bomber puzzle took a heavy toll on both he and his family. "But he must have forgotten he was shy several pieces of the puzzle with Stockton," DiPaolo said. "He cracked the case, the price of duty for an elite agent is becoming a legend in his own mind. He listened to that crackpot Marjorie Diehl-Armstrong who told him that Brian Wells was a willing participant. If she would have told this elite agent that her nitwit crew killed Jimmy Hoffa, he might have believed even that. The truth is that nobody will ever know of Wells' involvement."

In 2019, Tom Wolf was the Democratic Governor of Pennsylvania, the House of Representative and the Senate were controlled by the Republicans.

In early 2019 there were two seats on the ballot in Erie County for Common Plea Court Judges. Five Erie attorneys kicked off their campaigns to become judge.

Common Pleas Court Judge William "Rusty" Cunningham conveniently decided to retire right after the first of the year, so his seat could not be put on the ballot at the time.

Low and behold in June 2019, Marshall Piccinni was appointed to fill Cunningham's seat, while the other five attorneys were raising and speeding thousands and thousands of dollars campaigning to win one of the two seats. Piccinni comes off the street and puts on a robe. Republican politics at its worst. Cunningham, State Senator Dan Laughlin, and Piccinni pulled off the Caper of Capers.

DiPaolo and his friends and supporters who knew how the DiPaolos were treated by Piccinni and others with the purse party and Unicredit scam – were amazed by the political/judicial deal-making – but not surprised.

"When they've been getting away with these kind of activities for years, nothing is shocking," DiPaolo later said. "It was all a scam." Piccinni, who Dominick DiPaolo believes masterminded the raid on the DiPaolo home, along with his pal Foulk, was sworn in as Erie County Common Pleas judge on June 29, 2019. President Judge John Trucilla called Piccinni a man of great integrity. His buddy Cunningham said Piccinni has a profound respect for the law. And Laughlin also praised Piccinni for his integrity.

As DiPaolo viewed their comments, he came to the opinion that the three officials either lied or did not know what or who they were talking about. As well, Piccinni was praised for his efforts in the infamous so-called "Pizza Bomber Case," but then again, DiPaolo opined, the three either lied or didn't know that the case was mishandled by Piccinni and his F.B.I. pal, Jerry Clark.

"Although the Pizza Bomber case dates back to August 2003, some 17 years later, Palattella is still writing articles about it in the Erie Times-News," DiPaolo said. "I'm sure his best bud Pat Howard is letting him do it – talk about beating a dead horse."

DiPaolo pointed out that on July 5, 2020, Palattella penned a lengthy Page One article in the Sunday edition. The story included a large photo of his book partner, Jerry Clark, and the article discussed the deaths of Kenneth Barnes and Diehl of cancer in prison, "although perhaps millions of people die of cancer and I'm sure many prisoners do as well." The story went on to say that both Barnes and Diehl were buried as paupers and gave the section and plot numbers of each cemetery "in case Erie people want to visit them? Not the most creative journalism," DiPaolo said.

In addition, Diehl died in 2017 and Barnes in 2019. "But he could not do the story until 2020 as he had to wait for the information to come from a right-to-know request from the Bureau of Federal Prisons," DiPaolo said. No other news to report.

DiPaolo questioned why Palattella was still getting information on a 17-year-old closed murder case. "He's probably already written hundreds of stories about it, as he thinks Erie people really care? Or is it because he wants to keep selling his book? This is a perfect example of why the Erie Times is going under. They sold their building, shipped their printing out of town, and now have only a skeleton crew. It's employees like Palattella and Howard who are the reason Erie residents call it the 'Erie Rag,' – A front page story 17 years later on where two nitwits are buried. Plus, with early deadlines and the paper published out of town, nothing that happens after 7 p.m., even sports, gets in until two days later."

By late October 2020, Palattella was still writing about Marjorie Diehl, including one that said she was coloring between the lines when she was only seven years old and amazingly knew the difference between a dog and a hog, and a mouse and a house. Shouldn't all seven year olds know this? Wow, what a human interest story.

"Palattella, with his expert investigative techniques, found Diehl's first grade 1956 book "Fun in Phonics", with her name neatly printed on the cover, adding that nearly 50 years later she became a serial killer. I suggest the Gannett chain, which owns the Times Publishing Company, send Palattella to get checked out as it's been 17 years since the Pizza Bomber incident and he continues to write about Diehl, now we learn she colored between the lines as a seven-year-old," DiPaolo said. "I think Erie would also like to know who tagged her a serial killer? Ace Detective Jerry Clark? Again, misinformation to the public – a serial killer is someone who kills by themselves three or more people during their lifetime for abnormal psychological gratification. Crazy Margie doesn't fit that category."

As for Piccinni, who became a County Judge, DiPaolo said, "He has never conformed to the highest standards of character, impartiality, temperament and above all, honesty, credibility and integrity, even as a lawyer." Him lying to DiPaolo on the purse part raid is a good example.

When Piccinni was a U.S. Attorney in February 2017, the Feds indicted a suspect for dealing crack. The suspect could not make bail, and thus was incarcerated awaiting trial. By January 2018, the suspect filed a motion to dismiss the charges for violating the speedy trial rule. He never had a trial. The motion, however, was never answered by Piccinni. In the federal system, prosecutors have 70 days to bring suspects to trial unless there is an acceptable delay by the Feds or defendant. Since neither applied in this case, on December 21, 2020, nearly four years after the arrest, a Federal Judge ordered the crack dealer released from custody and dismissed the charges with prejudice, meaning the Feds cannot charge the suspect with the same crime ever again. "Imagine the job he will do as a Judge," DiPaolo speculated.

Attorney Christine Sanner, who was an Assistant U.S. Attorney in the Erie office under Piccinni, filed an Equal Employment Opportunity Commission complaint alleging a discrimination violation against the Erie office that Piccinni headed. Such a complaint is the first step in the filing of a federal law suit against an employer. Sanner had been the attorney assigned by Piccinni to the purse party raid at the DiPaolo home. "Piccinni and Foulk got mileage from Palattella in the News. But once it became public that that they were trying to destroy my reputation, Piccinni, who attended the raid in the shadows, bailed out of the case and assigned Sanner," DiPaolo said.

Sanner had told Attorney Tim Lucas that his client, the purse lady, did not have to give up her suppliers, those so-called terrorists, saying Piccinni advised, "Just stop doing parties. We are not interested in where they came from," according to DiPaolo.

DiPaolo located Sanner in 2019. A woman in her fifties, she was retired and living in Florida. When DiPaolo asked to talk with her about her role in the set-up purse raid scam, she replied, "I really would like to tell you about that case, but I settled my EEOC case and cannot disclose any prosecutions or investigations by the Erie office of the U.S. Attorney." She also told DiPaolo that she could not disclose the amount of her settlement, but DiPaolo guessed it was significant in that she is retired and enjoying the Florida sun.

"This should give the voters of Erie County a preview of what Piccinni is like and what his values are when he seeks their support," DiPaolo said. "He not only screwed over my family, but also screwed over his own co-worker – a woman for what, we can only surmise! Just think of how many others he can screw over as a Judge. Experience–Integrity–Justice? Yeah, right." Tell that to Brian Wells Family.

DiPaolo said it all sounds familiar with Republican politicians, "sticking up for their buddies." And doing whatever they want.

EPILOGUE

HERE ARE DiPAOLO'S THOUGHTS:

This book was written to set the record straight and expose the truth. Under the Rules of the Judicial Conduct board, it could not be written until Judge DiPaolo retired from the bench in 2018. On the purse party, the Feds had 168 pages in their investigative report. The Unicredit investigation had 1,724 pages of reports from the Feds and 3,000 pages of reports from the Office of the Attorney General. The Erie Times-News sensationalized both incidents for one reason, with over 100 articles to destroy DiPaolo, almost 5,000 pages of reports and probably thousands and thousands of man hours spending taxpayers' money for what? The purse lady, the scapegoat, got a slap on the hand, to make it look good and save face.

This book started with DiPaolo's background and the dedication he had to his community for many years. Then it shifted to what rats would try to do to him and his family.

What the Erie Times-News did to DiPaolo's family was similar to what rumors did in 1988 in the murder of Janine Kirk. Kirk was a beautiful young nurse who worked at Hamot Hospital. She was found dead at Presque Isle State Park's Beach #3 that June. The autopsy determined she died of blunt force trauma to her head and multiple stab wounds to her neck. The death was ruled a homicide. Rumors fueled by gossip, including talk radio, began to circulate that a Hamot Hospital doctor had been seeing the victim. It became the talk of Erie at social events, bars, clubs, anywhere people congregated. The doctor was named. The gossip was relentless, and even a morning talk show conducted a survey on whether the doctor did it.

It's a good thing there was no social media or Facebook at that time as all the nitwits would have made this doctor leave town. His practice and family suffered greatly. This went on for years, until in 2003, some 15 years later, Kirk's ex-boyfriend, Jamie Fleming, was arrested and convicted… and not the doctor. It was like during the 1950s when Republican U.S. Senator Joseph McCarthy falsely claimed government workers were Communists. It got so bad that the Republican Senate and his own people censored him. Or perhaps it was like the current Qanon, the sinister conspiracy of the Alex Jones Inforwards radio show hawking merchandise that allegedly can cure COVID-19 and cancer. His closest friend is Donald J. Trump – two nitwits trying to convince people of total falsehoods. But thousands of people believe them, just like they do a snake-oil salesmen.

"There is an entire book about conspiracies, people who believe in conspiracies which become impossible to disprove," DiPaolo points out. "People change facts by repeating and repeating falsehoods. Today, that's fueled by social media, letters, advertising. Even when people initially know it's not true, it's amplified over and over, drawing attention and then cannot be rebutted. This is a prime example with both the purse party and the Unicredit fiasco – it's how conspiracy theories grow and grow out of control by these rats. A perfect example is Donald Trump, who lied to the people day after day on many issues, his Republican minions knowing he was lying, but still went along with him. On Election Day 2020, he got 70 million votes from his wacko supporters who believed all his lies, and even now he is still stating that he won the election.

"Although he lost, he claimed fraud in the vote totals. Then his pathetic idiot, Attorney Rudy Giuliani filed law suits in different states in an attempt to change the vote, but they were thrown out as fast as they were filed. The only fraud was Trump, an embarrassment to himself and our country. Thank God for Joe Biden."

SILENCE IS COMPLICITY, as R. Gordon Kennedy often taught. He was Erie County's District Attorney in 1974 and a close friend of DiPaolo's. As he always told DiPaolo: "Remember that when the system fails, only righteous men will rise up." Kennedy died from cancer at 39 that year, but DiPaolo never forgot what he told him throughout his entire law enforcement and judicial career spanning 50 years.

DiPaolo is only trying to show how rumors fueled by inaccuracies and gossip, including articles written over and over, and then with social media and Facebook postings, causes misinformation that feeds on resentment, preconceptions, hatred and out and out lies. That these dishonest people post such fabrications, knowing nothing they are saying is true, is the real crime.

Between the purse party and the Unicredit scams, along with all the newspaper articles, DiPaolo was targeted in 2011 for his re-election with these many lies. But it did not work. In 2017, however, the same lies cost his daughter the election, with a group of low-lifes and dirt bags bringing up the purse party and Unicredit investigation and telling voters she was involved, which is a story in itself. DiPaolo, who has always been tough, but fair, with justice for all, and always tells it like it is.

This book is written in a very good year – January 25, 2020 marked the start of the Chinese New Year – The Year of the Rat. How apropos.